The ————— ...Practical Guide

This practical guide is intended for all clarinettists with a desire to investigate music of earlier periods. It contains practical help on both the acquisition and the playing of historical clarinets, while players of modern instruments will find much advice on style, approach and techniques which combine to make up a well-grounded period interpretation. The book presents and interprets evidence from primary sources and offers suggestions for further reading and investigation. Most importantly, a series of case studies which include the music of Handel, Mozart and Brahms helps recreate performances which will be as close as possible to the composer's original intention. As the early clarinet becomes increasingly popular worldwide, this guide, written by one of its foremost interpreters, will ensure that players at all levels – professional, students or amateurs – are fully aware of historical considerations in their performance.

COLIN LAWSON is one of Europe's leading period clarinettists. As principal clarinet of The English Concert, The Hanover Band and Collegium Musicum 90, he has recorded extensively and toured worldwide. An avid researcher into performance practice and the history of the clarinet, he is editor of *The Cambridge Companion to the Clarinet*, author of *Mozart: Clarinet Concerto* and *Brahms: Clarinet Quintet* in the series Cambridge Music Handbooks and co-author of *The Historical Performance of Music: An Introduction* in the present series. He currently holds the Chair of Performance Studies at Goldsmiths College in the University of London.

Cambridge Handbooks to the Historical Performance of Music

GENERAL EDITORS: Colin Lawson and Robin Stowell

During the last three decades historical performance has become part of mainstream musical life. However, there is as yet no one source from which performers and students can find an overview of the significant issues or glean practical information pertinent to a particular instrument. This series of handbooks guides the modern performer towards the investigation and interpretation of evidence found both in early performance treatises and in the mainstream repertory. Books on individual instruments contain chapters on historical background, equipment, technique and musical style and are illustrated by case studies of significant works in the repertoire. An introductory book provides a more general survey of issues common to all areas of historical performance and will also inform a wide range of students and music lovers.

Published titles

COLIN LAWSON AND ROBIN STOWELL *The Historical Performance of Music: An Introduction*

COLIN LAWSON *The Early Clarinet: A Practical Guide*

Forthcoming

JOHN HUMPHRIES *The Early Horn: A Practical Guide*

DAVID ROWLAND *Early Keyboard Instruments, 1550–1900: A Practical Guide*

ROBIN STOWELL *The Early Violin and Viola: A Practical Guide*

RACHEL BROWN *The Early Flute: A Practical Guide*

The Early Clarinet
A Practical Guide

Colin Lawson

PUBLISHED BY THE PRESS SYNDICATE OF THE UNIVERSITY OF CAMBRIDGE
The Pitt Building, Trumpington Street, Cambridge CB2 1RP, United Kingdom

CAMBRIDGE UNIVERSITY PRESS
The Edinburgh Building, Cambridge CB2 2RU, UK   http://www.cup.cam.ac.uk
40 West 20th Street, New York NY 10011-4211, USA   http://www.cup.org
10 Stamford Road, Oakleigh, Melbourne 3166, Australia

First published 2000

Printed in the United Kingdom at the University Press, Cambridge

Typeset in 10.25/14 Adobe Minion in QuarkXPress™   [SE]

A catalogue record for this book is available from the British Library

Library of Congress cataloguing in publication data
Lawson, Colin (Colin James)
The early clarinet: a practical guide / Colin Lawson.
        p.   cm. – (Cambridge handbooks to the historical performance of
music)
Includes biblographical references and index.
ISBN 0 521 62459 2 (hardback) – ISBN 0 521 62466 5 (paperback)
1. Clarinet music – 18th century – History and criticism.
2. Clarinet music – 19th century – History and criticism.
3. Performance practice (Music) – 18th century.   4. Performance
practice (Music) – 19th century.   5. Clarinet.   I. Title.
II. Series.
ML945.L39   2000
788.6'2'09033–dc21   99–32934   CIP

ISBN 0 521 62459 2 hardback
ISBN 0 521 62466 5 paperback

Contents

Illustrations

Acknowledgements for kind permission to reproduce illustrations
are due to the Bibliothèque Nationale (Fig. 3.1) and the British
Library (Fig. 7.1).

Preface

This practical guide is intended for all clarinet devotees with an interest in historical performance, whether as professionals, students, enthusiastic concert-goers, discriminating listeners or players of modern instruments seeking advice about those matters of style, approach and general technique which combine to make up a well-grounded period interpretation. The art of music is indeed notoriously difficult to describe in words, and there were inevitably numerous conventions which theorists simply took for granted. However, primary sources can be a great inspiration, whether on a philosophical or a practical level. Above all, we should never forget that in Mozart's day the performer's foremost aim was to move an audience.

Treatises can illuminate the history of music in a variety of unexpected ways. For example, Joseph Fröhlich's *Vollständige theoretisch-praktische Musikschule* (Bonn, 1810–11) has the following advice for the wind-player. He recommends a moderate life-style and avoidance of anything which could damage the chest, such as running, riding on horseback or excessive indulgence in hot drinks. One should not practise after a meal and so the afternoon is best avoided; furthermore, one should not drink immediately after practising if the lungs are still warm, since this has been the cause of early deaths with many people. In the case of dry lips – very bad for the embouchure – the mouth should be rinsed, preferably with an alcoholic beverage to give the lips new strength. Crucially, Fröhlich's advice needs to be interpreted with the original conditions and tastes in mind, since he was writing at a time when a performer's continued good health was an altogether more fragile matter than it is today.

The primary aim of this book is to present and interpret evidence from such sources on matters which include technique, style and expression, and to offer suggestions for further reading and investigation. There is also guidance on many other relevant issues, as well as advice regarding the acquisition of appropriate instruments and accessories. The parent volume to the series, *The Historical Performance of Music: An Introduction* (co-authored by the present writer with Robin Stowell), deals with the more general, large-scale practical issues that need to be addressed in connection with the preparation and execution of performances which are historically informed, yet at the same time individual and vivid. It happens that one of its case studies is Mozart's magnificent Serenade K361 for thirteen instruments, a cornerstone in the repertory of any clarinettist or basset horn player.

For the series as a whole, the core study period is *c*. 1700–*c*. 1900, a time-span within which most important developments in the history of the clarinet took place. Each of the volumes includes a number of case studies, demonstrating the application of the technical, interpretative and other principles discussed in different performing situations and in various musical genres. In Chapter 6 will be found discussion of specific works by Handel, Stamitz, Mozart, Weber and Brahms. This is intended to provide an historical basis for artistic decision-making which has as its goal the re-creation of a performance as close as possible to the composer's original conception.

My own experience of playing early clarinets has been stimulating on a variety of levels. Primarily, I believe that engagement with original conditions has the capacity radically to expand one's musical horizons. Of course, different historical clarinets present satisfying technical challenges and their variety of response is pleasurable both on a purely physical and on an aesthetic level. In particular, I believe that the variety and range of nuance available from many early clarinets is well-nigh impossible to match on the modern Boehm instrument. Many years ago, as a novice of the early clarinet, I fell into the trap of supposing that period instruments were somehow more difficult to play, even within their own particular repertory, an argument I should now find it difficult to sustain. As historical performance has become more widespread, the sheer popularity of the modern clarinet has filtered down to early instruments at the hands of players from various backgrounds. Inevitably, some fine players of Boehm-system clarinets are content to overload their early clarinets with mechanism and to pay scant attention to considerations of style. As will be emphasised in the following chapters, an approach which merely allows practical expediency to predominate is bound to be limited in its aspirations and achievements.

It is a pleasure to thank a number of friends and colleagues for their help and advice in the preparation of this book. Having lost both my parents during the gestation of this project, I am acutely aware that my own interest in the clarinet was originally begun, sustained and nourished with their unstinting support. After initial academic interest in the history of the chalumeau and early clarinet, I was first inspired to complementary practical endeavours by collaborations on Spanish concert platforms with my friend and erstwhile pupil, Carles Riera. Later immersion in period performance brought me into close contact with Nicholas Shackleton, who has always been generous enough to place at my disposal his unrivalled knowledge of surviving instruments world-wide. The Cambridge maker Daniel Bangham alerted me to the expressive potential of boxwood clarinets by producing for me many fine copies from different eras of the instrument's history. I am also grateful to Ingrid Pearson for writing Chapter 4 and for innumerable other important details in the text. Last but not least, Penny Souster at Cambridge University Press has been characteristically tactful in creating that sense of urgency which no publication can afford to be without during each stage of its preparation.

In the following chapters, pitch registers are indicated in the following manner: middle C just below the treble staff is indicated as c', with each successive octave higher shown as c', c'', c'''' etc. and the octave below as c. For fingerings, L = left hand, R = right hand, th = thumb and finger 1 = index.

1   The early clarinet in context

Introduction

Many clarinettists today are familiar with various different types of historical clarinet which have been consistently illustrated in books and journals. Nowadays these instruments are regularly being played throughout the world, giving a quite new perspective to the art of clarinet performance. The various designs of early clarinet will not be reproduced here, since a representative selection is already accessible within the pages of *The Cambridge Companion to the Clarinet* (Cambridge University Press, 1995).

During the course of little more than a generation, period performance has indeed become part of mainstream musical life and is pursued with skill and dedication by an ever-increasing circle of performers. Opportunities now exist to commission copies of various types of early clarinets and to perform a wide range of repertory using instruments which would have been familiar to the composers themselves. Given sufficient dedication, any experienced and open-minded modern player can achieve technical command over a wide range of clarinets. An encouragement to initiative here is Joseph Fröhlich's observation from 1810: 'Owing to the different construction and various manners of blowing wind and reed instruments, there are no generally applicable rules of fingering. All one can do is give the usual fingerings and a critique on each note, and, at the same time, to inform the student of the various manners in which the same note can be fingered, in order to make the dark notes brighter and more sonorous, and to improve the bad ones. Consequently, one must really see to it that each player evolves the fingering for himself.'[1]

In 1752 the flautist Quantz set out to train a skilled and intelligent musician, remarking that the majority of players had fingers and tongues, but that most were deficient in brains! At the same period C. P. E. Bach warned that players whose chief asset was mere technique were clearly at a disadvantage. Both writers emphasise that if a player is not himself moved by what he plays he will never move others, which should be his real aim. In our own very different musical climate it is easy to become embarrassed by such sentiments, but in Mozart's day – well before the enthusiasm for virtuosity as an end in itself during the nineteenth century or the veneration for accuracy which has developed during the age of recording – the communication of emotion was an absolute priority. For today's specialist in period performance, the acquisition of instruments and even the technique to play them can only be the starting point; the whole exercise will be severely limited unless harnessed to a feeling for appropriate musical styles. Quantz described music as 'nothing but an artificial language, through which we seek to acquaint the listener with our musical ideas'.[2] This analogy with oratory implies a range of articulation far removed from the goals of many modern clarinettists, who arguably have moved further in the direction of a smooth, seamless approach than most flautists, oboists or bassoonists.

Historical performance and the clarinet

The upsurge of interest in the early clarinet has made it a subject worthy of specialist study and it is now routinely available as a principal subject at the main conservatoires. But only a few years ago, it would have seemed inconceivable that there could be any apparent advantage in resurrecting clarinets from pre-Boehm days. As late as 1980 the article 'performing practice' in *The New Grove Dictionary* could still claim that repertory after 1750 involves no lost tradition: 'there has been no severance of contact with post-Baroque music as a whole, nor with the instruments used in performing it . . . To hear Beethoven's symphonies played with the same degree of authenticity [as the Horn Sonata] would be no less revealing in sound quality, but the practical difficulties of assembling and equipping such an orchestra are almost insuperable.' Subsequent musical revelations proved such an argument untenable, as period interpretations of Mozart and Beethoven symphonies moved well past the experimental stage, to widespread acclamation. Cycles of Haydn, Mendelssohn, Schumann and even Brahms then gave an enormous impetus to study of the early clarinet, once period orchestral repertory had broken through an artificial divide of 1750.

The movement which was to ignite a smouldering interest in the early clarinet is recounted by Harry Haskell in his book *The Early Music Revival*

(London, 1988). His narrative appraises the activities of musicologists, editors, publishers, makers, collectors, curators, dealers, librarians, performers, teachers and record producers. Haskell shows that baroque music was indeed for a long time the latest period to be examined with a scholarly eye. Indeed, he begins his narrative with Mendelssohn's revival in 1829 of Bach's *St Matthew Passion* , in which the orchestra was updated to include clarinets, in the absence of oboi d'amore and da caccia. Eventually at the end of the nineteenth century there began the reproduction of early instruments, initially keyboards, strings and eventually recorders.

Prior to 1939, period performance was well represented in the pre-war recording studio, though generally by renaissance and baroque repertory. The immediate post-war period witnessed recordings of an ever-increasing amount of baroque music. Among projects undertaken (on modern instruments) by Karl Haas and the London Baroque Ensemble were Handel's *Ouverture* for two clarinets and horn and Vivaldi's Concerto RV559 for pairs of oboes and clarinets. The early clarinet was the last of the woodwinds to enter the recording studio. A pioneering venture was the 1969 recording (for Telefunken) of Beethoven's Trio Op. 11 by Piet Honingh, using a five-keyed instrument by Jung of Marseilles. In the 1970s the growing number of period baroque ensembles was supplemented by the Collegium Aureum founded by Franzjosef Maier, which recorded much classical chamber music involving clarinet (played by Hans Deinzer on a generously mechanized boxwood instrument), as well as the first period version of the Mozart Clarinet Concerto in 1973. With the Academy of Ancient Music, Christopher Hogwood moved into later territory than he had inhabited in David Munrow's Early Music Consort; his early projects included symphonies by Arne, as well as the Clarinet Concerto by Johann Stamitz, with Alan Hacker as soloist. Hacker brought an enthusiasm for early instruments to the classical repertory, notably with his own group The Music Party, introducing period performance of music from 1760 to 1830 to a wide public at a time when such projects were scarcely known at all. During the 1970s opportunities in Britain to hear original instruments at first hand became more frequent, for example with the arrival of the Bate Collection in Oxford, a working collection complementing instruments on display at the Horniman Museum and at the Royal College of Music in London, and in Edinburgh's Reid Collection.

Classical performance on a larger scale entered a new era in the early 1980s, with Hogwood's project to record Mozart's complete symphonies. Once they had been recorded on historical instruments, it could soon be demonstrated that the clarinet concertos of Mozart and Weber were idiomatically suited to the kinds of instrument for which they were originally intended. As historical activity spread from the principal and distinctive centres such as England and Holland, many established baroque conductors broadened their horizons to include the classical period. The widespread reproduction of keyboard instruments was followed by flutes and double reeds and eventually led to various makers offering fine copies of early clarinets. The finite number of surviving originals has ensured that replicas are encountered ever more frequently, and this is assuredly something of a loss because (as we shall find later in this book) copies can easily be tuned and customised in a way which emphasises modern as well as period characteristics.

Clarinet literature

In general, historical matters have attracted a much greater clarinet literature than technique or the application of style. The instrument has been the subject of lively discussion in musical journals ever since the time of Mozart. In the early nineteenth century important German periodicals such as the *Allgemeine musikalische Zeitung* and *Cäcilia* devoted attention to it. A couple of generations later, the first edition of *Grove's Dictionary of Music* included a wide-ranging article on the clarinet which enumerated its various characteristics and difficulties; it is discussed in detail in Chapter 2. There were complete books devoted to the clarinet in Italian (1887) and German (1904),[3] and then in 1916 came an important historical survey from the English amateur Oscar Street.[4] The change in the clarinet's status since that time is revealed by Street's observation, 'the [Mozart] Concerto is alas! very seldom heard nowadays. I find that it has not been played at a Philharmonic Concert since Willman played it in 1838, and as a Fellow of that honourable old Society I should like to place on record my regret at the neglect of such a beautiful work. I have only heard it played once in its entirety, and that was by Mr. Charles Draper in the early days of the Beecham orchestra . . .'

Adam Carse's general book on wind instruments from 1939 contains a celebrated (if then accurate) description of the chalumeau as 'this will' o th' wisp of wind instruments'.[5] A post-war landmark was Anthony Baines's *Woodwind Instruments and their History* of 1957, which deals separately with the mechanical and practical aspects of playing modern and historical woodwinds. Its distinctive and far-sighted text includes a fingering chart for the simple-system clarinet. Geoffrey Rendall's article in the fifth edition of *Grove* also compared Boehm and Albert systems on an equal footing: 'the Boehm player circumvents difficulties by nimbleness of mind, by selecting the most convenient among several possible fingerings, the old system player by nimbleness of finger in sliding from key to key.'[6] Rendall's book on the clarinet (published in 1954) dealt with both practical and historical matters, usefully illustrating a variety of early clarinets. Meanwhile, *The Galpin Society Journal* contained from its beginnings in 1948 a steady stream of articles of interest to clarinettists by R. B. Chatwin, Thurston Dart, Horace Fitzpatrick, Eric Halfpenny, Roger Hellyer, Edgar Hunt, J. H. Van der Meer and others. Oskar Kroll, who had already undertaken important research into the chalumeau, wrote a book on the clarinet published in 1965 (English translation 1968), which had been in preparation as early as 1939.[7] Kroll brought an important German perspective to the history and repertory of the clarinet. A different, more comprehensive view was offered within a scholarly three-part article (1958) in the German encyclopaedia *Die Musik in Geschichte und Gegenwart*, covering acoustics, ethnic and ancient clarinet types and the European clarinet. Of its three authors, Heinz Becker also published independent articles elsewhere on the eighteenth-century clarinet and on the chalumeau.

Pamela Weston's *Clarinet Virtuosi of the Past* (London, 1971) and *More Clarinet Virtuosi of the Past* (London, 1977) introduced both a biographical and a critical perspective on earlier performers. Jack Brymer's book *Clarinet* (London, 1976) included some valuable historical information for the general reader, as well as some useful photographs of early instruments. His enthusiastic remarks about the early clarinet reflected its then gradual emergence on to the musical scene. More specifically relevant in the present context is Nicholas Shackleton's *New Grove* article 'clarinet', revised in 1984 for *The New Grove Dictionary of Musical Instruments*, whose illustrations include early reeds and mouthpieces. The clarinet has remained a popular subject for university theses, and David Ross's 'A Comprehensive Performance Project in Clarinet Literature with an Organological Study of the Development of the Clarinet in the Eighteenth Century' (University of Iowa, 1985) is worth investigating for its many descriptions of surviving old clarinets. Albert Rice's *The Baroque Clarinet* (1992) takes an essentially bibliographical approach to an as yet under-researched area. A few clarinet tutors are currently available in facsimile and they are listed, together with most of the books and articles mentioned here, in the *Bibliography of the Early Clarinet* (Brighton, 1986) compiled by Jo Rees-Davies. More recent advice on the technique of playing early clarinets has been concentrated in the journal articles listed in the bibliography, whilst *The Cambridge Companion to the Clarinet* (Cambridge, 1995) includes a chapter by the present author entitled 'Playing historical clarinets'. *Early Music* (from 1973) continues to be an important forum for makers, players, and scholars and authors. Venturing into single-reed territory with increasing regularity, it has included articles on practical concerns by players or scholars such as David Charlton, Eric Hoeprich and Albert Rice. Significantly, it has frequently contained discussion of performance practice issues of direct relevance to clarinettists.

The collector

By comparison with a period string player, the clarinettist must perforce have an extensive collection of instruments . An investigation of the baroque repertory will involve four sizes of chalumeaux, two-keyed clarinets in C and D for Handel and Vivaldi and a later design of D clarinet for the Molter concertos. Within the classical period, Mozart's music alone will require Viennese clarinets in A, B♭, B and C, as well as basset clarinets in B♭ and A and basset horn in F.[8] One might also like to have English instruments for repertory such as Mahon or Hook and French instruments for Lefèvre and his compatriots. The early Romantic solo repertory by Weber or Spohr and orchestral parts by Beethoven or Mendelssohn need to be played on a more powerful type of ten- or twelve-keyed clarinet. Again, clarinets in A, B♭ and C will be required and there is an important distinction to be made between German and French designs. For Berlioz, authentic thirteen-keyed

French clarinets are indispensable. When the Boehm system first appeared, clarinets were for a time still being manufactured in boxwood. This is also the material of Richard Mühlfeld's Baermann-Ottensteiner clarinets on which the Brahms chamber works were premièred. Cocuswood was another popular medium, especially for the Albert- (simple-) system clarinets which found special favour in Britain until the inter-war era.

Evidence of various kinds indicates that the clarinet was originally far less standardised than we can imagine. Reeds and mouthpieces are areas where historical propriety and practical convenience need to be delicately balanced; experiments and research of one's own are preferable merely to following current fashion. Relatively few mouthpieces survive intact, even where the clarinet is in good condition. A wide variety of mouthpiece designs existed, often with much smaller slots than we are used to, frequently with a very close lay (though not always surviving in original condition) and usually requiring a reed which is quite narrow and shorter at the base than its modern counterpart. Historical mouthpieces and reeds are discussed in later chapters. The reed was tied on to the mouthpiece with twine until Müller's espousal of the metal ligature near the beginning of the nineteenth century.[9]

Style

Playing different types of early clarinet offers a stimulating artistic and technical experience which can inspire a fresh approach to the modern instrument. Arguably, the very design of the Boehm instrument has encouraged a tonal homogeneity which has diminished the clarinet's character and rhetorical potential. As we have already noted, historical equipment and even technique can only be the first step towards investigating the sound-world of earlier composers. Real understanding of a composer's full expressive range implies an acquaintance with the musical *language* of the time. In recent years the relatively young discipline of performance practice has become a lively subject for debate. Clearly, there was much that a composer did not trouble to write into his scores; he simply expected certain conventions to be observed. Some of these simply no longer exist, while others have undergone significant changes of meaning. Using a clarinet for which a particular repertory was originally intended can make the music sound more expressive and can make more sense of what the composer actually wrote.

Interpreting the evidence

The very ambiguity of historical evidence means that there will always be more questions than answers. The issues addressed in the central chapters of the parent volume to the present series are all generally applicable to the clarinet repertory to a greater or lesser degree.[10] Thus the application of primary sources involves examination of surviving instruments, as well as iconographical sources, historical archives and literary sources. Treatises for instruments such as violin, flute or keyboards offer philosophical insights into the art and craft of music and make essential reading for any musician wishing to develop a historical perspective. Musical styles are many and various, with national idiom an important element. Specific areas for detailed study include articulation, melodic inflection, accentuation, tempo, rhythmic alteration, ornamentation, extempore embellishment and improvisation. Furthermore, the interpretation of notation implies a knowledge of conditions and practices for which even an autograph score may offer no clues. These might include such central issues as pitch and temperament, constitution of original programmes, orchestral disposition and placement and the role (if any) of the conductor.

The current scene

As performance standards have risen sharply, it has become less fashionable to claim that early music groups are filled with performers who failed to make the grade in the mainstream musical world. It must be admitted that technical facility was grossly undervalued in the early music market a few years ago, but what makes the criticism bite is that early musicians originally prided themselves on being more adventurous and readier to question received opinions. The whole concept of period performance was subjected to detailed scrutiny in a series of articles in *Early Music* in 1984, revised for inclusion in Nicholas Kenyon's penetrating symposium *Authenticity and Early Music* (Oxford, 1988). In his provocative series of essays *Baroque Music Today* Nikolaus Harnoncourt ascribes the

development of the entire movement to the unhealthy artistic environ-
ment of today: 'the unwillingness to bring [historical music] into the
present, but rather to return oneself to the past . . . is a symptom of the loss
of a truly living contemporary music . . . This kind of historical perspective
is totally alien to a culturally vital period.'[11] Whatever the degree of truth
here, early instruments have above all made musicians think about style in
a constructive way, with some spectacular results already applied to
'modern' ensembles.

2 Historical considerations

Aims and aspirations

Is the kind of performance expected by a composer in his own day valid for later generations of players? We can never really answer this question, if only because life has changed so much during the last couple of centuries. The importance of the microphone in our musical lives and the various implications of air travel are two factors which have brought about such changes that we do not really have the option to turn back the clock. Even if we could hear Anton Stadler's première of Mozart's Clarinet Concerto in 1791, we should not necessarily want to adopt all its features; in other words, like all period performers from our own time, we would be bound to exercise elements of choice and taste as much characteristic of the twentieth century as of the eighteenth.[1]

The value of knowledge to complement musical taste has been recognised by generations of composers and performers. The nature and disposition of the clarinet repertory poses some stylistic special problems for even the most receptive of players. We clarinettists lack the opportunity to cultivate a well-honed baroque performance style from which to formulate a classical mode of expression, whilst in the nineteenth century there is no significant body of sonatas in the period immediately preceding the Brahms works from which to formulate a mature interpretation. In more general terms, the history of music is strewn with instances of poor performing conditions which we shall not want to emulate; but the single fact that detached, articulated playing was the norm in Mozart's day is a sufficient reminder of the way in which performance styles have changed out of all recognition. The Boehm clarinet which we all know so well was designed (a mere fifty years after Mozart's death) for a very different kind of music. Nicholas Kenyon asked his contributors to *Authenticity and Early Music* to consider whether a composer's music was likely to be better understood by restricting resources to the means he had available when he wrote it, or whether such a restriction

10

inhibited its full expression. In respect of this last question a number of clar-inettists would prefer to argue that for Mozart or Weber it is the Boehm clar-inet which represents the restriction rather than the type of instrument contemporary with the composer.

Origin and development of the clarinet

As we noted in the previous chapter, the remarkable and eventful history of the clarinet has been the subject of a substantial number of books and articles. The earliest years of any instrument's life inevitably reveal varied patterns of acceptance, and only gradually is any coherent picture of the early eighteenth-century clarinet beginning to emerge. However, any lingering doubts about the clarinet's vigorous career in the two generations before Mozart's birth have now at last been conclusively laid to rest.[2] It is the special acoustical make-up of the clarinet which seems to account for many particular features of its history. For example, during the first half century of its life it really existed as two instruments; the essence of the baroque clarinet was its upper register, whereas its close relative the chalumeau was restricted to the range of a twelfth in its fundamental register. Only during the classical period did it become possible to manufacture an instrument in which both registers were relatively satisfactory and in tune. The four sizes of chalumeau find a place in the catalogues of most modern makers, even though the rep-ertory remains largely unpublished. Enthusiasm for the instrument in Vienna throughout much of the eighteenth century is nicely encapsulated in Daniel Schubart's book on aesthetics, where he belatedly wrote that 'its tone is so interesting, so individual and so endlessly pleasant that the whole world of music would suffer a grievous loss if the instrument ever fell into disuse'.[3]

Although single-reed instruments in folk music have routinely been traced back at least as far as *c.* 3000 BC, there is remarkably no evidence of clarinet-types in notated art music until about AD 1700. There has never been any real evidence to contradict the Nuremberg writer J. G. Doppelmayr, who in 1730 ascribed the birth of the clarinet and the improve-ment of the chalumeau to Johann Christoph Denner.[4] Doppelmayr was not always wholly reliable, tended to exaggerate the achievements of local crafts-men, and did not trouble to investigate the contributions of other makers to the development of the chalumeau or the clarinet. But the most serious problem is that he failed to make clear the exact relationship of the two instruments, though his information can be supplemented from treatises such as Bonanni (*Gabinetto Armonico,* Rome 1722), Walther (*Musikalisches Lexicon,* Leipzig 1732) and Majer (*Museum musicum,* Schwäbisch Hall 1732). Musical sources show that the soprano, alto, tenor and bass sizes of two-keyed chalumeau described by Majer had as their lowest note f', c', f and c respectively. The name chalumeau suggests French origin, and perhaps even some connection with the Hotteterre family, who during the seventeenth century were celebrated makers of recorders, flutes, oboes and bassoons. In 1696 J. C. Denner and the woodwind maker Johann Schell petitioned the Nuremberg city council to be recognised as master craftsmen and to be granted leave to make for sale 'the French musical instruments . . .which were invented about twelve years ago [i. e. in 1684] in France'.[5] Only the recorder and oboe are actually mentioned in this successful petition, but the chalumeau was probably one of the new instruments. Documentary evidence of the clarinet dates only from the year 1710.[6]

The chalumeau and its music

The soprano chalumeau, equivalent in size to sopranino recorder, is an obvious starting point for studying the instrument, since the entire Viennese repertory was composed for it. The chalumeau became a favourite obbligato instrument in Vienna during the early years of the eighteenth century, notably in the operas and oratorios of the Kapellmeister Johann Joseph Fux (1660–1741).[7] It often appears as an alternative to the oboe, either in pairs or with flute or recorder in pastoral or amorous scenes, foreshadowing Mozart's use of the clarinet in *Così fan tutte.* Regular obbligato appearances until the 1730s in the works of contemporary composers such as Ariosti, Bonno, A. M. and G. Bononcini, Caldara, Conti, Porsile and Reutter remain largely undiscovered. However, a modern facsimile of cantatas by Conti includes his chalumeau obbligati, whilst two of Giovanni Bononcini's arias have been published in an edition with clarinet, together with an aria written by the Emperor Joseph I for insertion in Ziani's *Chilonida* of 1709. Most celebrated of all orchestral contexts with chalumeau are the Viennese versions of Gluck's *Orfeo* (1762) and *Alceste* (1767), showing the instrument's continued profile much later.

Remarkably, there were dramatic works with chalumeau from a yet later period; the Bohemian Gassmann included it in *I rovinati* (1772) during the last year of his life; in the previous year Starzer had used a pair in his ballet *Roger et Bradamante*. Starzer composed an especially significant piece of chamber music for two chalumeaux or flutes, five trumpets and timpani, written during the period 1760–8 when he was leader of the orchestra at St Petersburg. Not long afterwards, Mozart's father copied out all five movements, specifying flutes for the upper parts. Arrangements of three numbers from Gluck's *Paris ed Elena* were added, and the eight movements were subsequently catalogued as Mozart's K187, later 159c, before their true identity was revealed in 1937.[8] Gassmann's *Notturno* and Dittersdorf's *Divertimento notturno* (as yet unpublished) provide certain evidence of the survival of the chalumeau into the Viennese classical period.[9] An even more tempting prospect is the concerto for 'schalamaux' by Hoffmeister (1754–1812), with its appropriately light scoring; the work presumably pre-dates his exploration of the clarinet, but nevertheless surely belongs no earlier than the 1770s. Of other repertory for soprano chalumeau, the virtuoso concerto (*c.* 1730) by Fasch is currently available in print,[10] whilst Vivaldi's oratorio *Juditha triumphans* (1716) contains a poignant obbligato in an aria concerning the lament of a turtle-dove.

Telemann continued to use a pair of alto and tenor chalumeaux long after he had first employed the clarinet in a cantata of 1721. Three of his chalumeau works are available in a modern edition – the fine D minor double concerto, featuring an unusual degree of unaccompanied chromatic writing, the suite in F for two chalumeaux and/or *violette* and continuo, and the extraordinary *Grillen-Symphonie*, scored for flute or piccolo, oboe, alto chalumeau, two double basses, strings and continuo. Christoph Graupner, second choice after Telemann for Bach's post at Leipzig, was the most prolific composer for the chalumeau, including it in over eighty cantatas during 1734–53, and in eighteen instrumental works. The two suites for alto, tenor and bass chalumeaux have been published, as has Graupner's unusually scored trio for bass chalumeau, bassoon and cello. Indeed, Graupner is the only documented composer for bass chalumeau.[11]

A complete listing of chalumeau repertoire would also include works by a variety of composers, such as J. L. Bach, Harrer, Hasse, König, Molter, Schürmann, Steffani, von Wilderer and Zelenka, amongst numerous others.

An exquisite obbligato occurs in Handel's opera *Riccardo Primo*. Composed in the spring of 1727 for performance at the end of the 1726–7 season, the première was in the event postponed until November of that year. Originally Handel had written an aria ('Quando non vede') with two obbligato chalumeau parts; these must have been intended for the visiting German clarinet players August Freudenfeld and Francis Rosenberg, who had been in London for about two years and had held benefit concerts in March 1726 and March 1727. Unfortunately, it seems that they left London in the summer of 1727 and so as part of his pre-performance revisions of the opera Handel had to re-write the aria, replacing the chalumeaux with oboes. The text was also somewhat revised.[12]

Baroque clarinet repertory

Rice's *The Baroque Clarinet* lists some twenty-eight works by as many as thirteen composers. Nevertheless, the focus of attention for modern players of the two-keyed clarinet is likely to remain Handel, Vivaldi and Molter, even though orchestral C or D clarinet parts have been found in the works of Caldara (1718), Conti (1719), J. A. J. Faber (1720), Telemann (1721, 1728) and Graupner (final cantata, 1754). The Handel *Ouverture* for two D clarinets and horn from the 1740s, perhaps an open-air piece, forms one of the case studies in Chapter 6. Two of Vivaldi's concertos, RV559 and RV560, are scored for pairs of oboes and C clarinets and, besides a lively appreciation of the upper register, show a delight in exploiting the lugubrious qualities of the lower register, emphasised by the use of minor-key inflections. These various colours are much more evident with period instruments. The difference in timbre between the two registers was subsequently noted by the German author Adlung in 1758, who stated: 'The clarinet is well known. In the low register it sounds differently from the high range, and therefore one calls it chalumeau.'[13] A third Vivaldi concerto with clarinets 'per la Solennità di San Lorenzo' combines aspects of the solo concerto with concerto grosso, incorporating a large wind section with recorders, oboes, clarinets ('clareni') and bassoon.[14] The Molter concertos are technically the most advanced for the baroque clarinet, consistently employing the tessitura between c''' and g''', with notes below c'' usually triadic only.

The leaps, ornamental figuration, flourishes and chromatic inflections have been discussed and tabulated by Rice, whose musical examples give a clear idea of Molter's idioms. The principal sources of playing technique for this period are books by Majer and Eisel, which contain (not wholly reliable) fingering charts.[15]

Classical

As the cantabile qualities of the clarinet began to be reflected in its design, the five-keyed instrument was developed, its principal registers balanced and tuned in such a way as to make the chalumeau redundant as a separate entity. The first concerto for B♭ clarinet is probably that ascribed to Johann Stamitz (d. 1757), which forms one of the case studies in Chapter 6; numerous other composers of the Mannheim school made important contributions to clarinet repertory, notably Stamitz's son Karl. Of the many tutors for the classical clarinet, Lefèvre and Backofen offer a great deal of sound technical advice and are readily accessible in modern reprints.[16] French sonatas by Devienne and Lefèvre were originally written with a mere bass line as accompaniment; they contrast with the more fully realised Viennese sonatas of Hoffmeister and Vanhal. Technique was also sharply differentiated by nationality, with the French continuing the practice of playing with reed against the top lip at a time when the Austro-German tradition had apparently already switched to reed below.[17] Naturally, it is Mozart's music which lies at the heart of most discussions of the classical clarinet. His use of Anton Stadler's newly developed basset clarinet (as it has become known) for the Quintet and Concerto poses various problems of text and equipment which have been the subject of recent debate and have attracted a substantial literature.[18] Significantly, an important contemporary appreciation of Stadler's playing claimed that his instrument had so soft and lovely a tone that no-one with a heart could resist it.[19] At exactly the same time Schubart characterised the clarinet as overflowing with love, with an indescribable sweetness of expression. When Stadler was asked in 1800 to design a syllabus for a music school he insisted that every music student should learn basic principles through singing, whatever the quality of his voice.[20] Although Lefèvre's tutor addresses such matters as the distinctive characterisation of Allegro and Adagio movements, the classical style is much more fully documented elsewhere, notably in the *Clavierschule* by Daniel Gottlob Türk, who was well acquainted with Mozart's music.[21]

Romantic

As we have already suggested, the later symphonies of Beethoven, together with chamber works by such composers as Burgmüller, Danzi, Mendelssohn and Weber require a more powerful, flexible instrument and a performance philosophy to match. For expanding one's knowledge of little-known repertory (in which the early nineteenth century is especially rich) major clarinet bibliographies such as those by Opperman, Brixel and Dobrée can be a useful starting point.[22] Some adventurous clarinettists have ventured to European libraries to investigate little-known material; among interesting duo repertory unearthed in Vienna are the sonatas by Anton Eberl and Caroline Schleicher (née Krähmer).

The sheer diversity of approaches to clarinet playing at this time can be comprehended from the documentary evidence. Iwan Müller's thirteen-keyed clarinet was promoted in 1812 as omnitonic; although this claim was in any event somewhat exaggerated, his clarinet was resisted at the Paris Conservatoire on the grounds that it eliminated desirable tonal distinctions between clarinets in different keys. Nevertheless, its design proved highly influential. An important appreciation of the French thirteen-keyed clarinet occurs in Berlioz's orchestration treatise.[23] Müller's clarinet was subject to refinements by the Belgian Adolphe Sax and was further developed by Carl Baermann in association with the Munich manufacturer Georg Ottensteiner. Baermann's tutor represents a forward-looking, intelligent approach to the instrument.[24] All repertory associated with the Brahms circle is appropriate for this design, including the Schumann *Fantasiestücke*, which were a favourite of Mühlfeld.[25] The Meiningen orchestra in which he played comprised a mere forty-nine players and must have produced a relatively soft-edged sound.

The so-called simple- (or Albert-) system clarinet popular in England until the inter-war period is a further variant of the thirteen-keyed design. Much of the burgeoning English repertory which followed in the wake of Brahms must have been performed on such instruments.[26] It cannot be sufficiently emphasised that the Boehm system in popular use today lies outside these traditions. This instrument was first exhibited in 1843, devised by the clarinettist Hyacinthe Klosé with the maker Auguste Buffet *jeune* and representing a radical re-thinking of the instrument in that the fundamental scale is produced by raising successive fingers, eliminating forked fingerings which were a feature of all previous (and most subsequent) clarinets.[27]

A snapshot from 1879

The article 'clarinet' in the first volume of *Grove's Dictionary of Music and Musicians* (vol. I, London, 1879, pp. 361–4) offers an important British perspective on the clarinet little more than a decade before Brahms's chamber music for the instrument. Like the other woodwind articles, the text was written by Dr W. H. Stone, a physician. Introducing his discussion of the older and more usual form (i.e. simple-system), he claimed that 'Boehm or Klosé's fingering is hardly so well adapted to this as to the octave-scaled instruments. It certainly removes some difficulties, but at the expense of greatly increased complication of mechanism, and liability to get out of order.' One can appreciate that aspects of the Boehm system such as the left-hand thumb mechanism must initially have appeared elaborate. Discussion as to whether musical instruments had improved or merely changed was rife during the great technological developments of the nineteenth century.[28] Amidst all the argument, some felt that the new versatility of wind instruments was indispensable, whereas others believed that something of the individuality of tone-colour was lost as a result of mechanical developments. Stone felt that the true qualities of older instruments were being abandoned, remarking in another of his articles that 'hardly any instrument, except the flute, has been so altered and modified . . . in its mechanism . . . as the oboe . . . It has thus become by far the most elaborate and complicated of reed instruments, and it is a question whether a return to an older and simpler pattern, by lessening the weight of the machine, and the number of holes breaking the continuity of the bore, and by increasing the vibratory powers of the wooden tube, would not conduce to an improved quality of tone.'[29] From his writings as a whole it seems probable that more than a century ago Stone would have heartily approved of the return to period instruments for baroque and classical repertory.

Stone's article on the clarinet also illustrates the serious individual problems brought about by the new challenges in orchestral music. He describes the end of the first movement of Beethoven's 'Pastoral' Symphony as 'singularly trying to the player', while 'few players can execute with absolute correctness' the trio of the Eighth. He regards a notorious passage in Mendelssohn's Scherzo from *A Midsummer Night's Dream* (bars 131–3) as 'all but unplayable'. In Rossini's overtures *Semiramide, Otello* and *Gazza ladra* , 'the difficulties assigned to it [the clarinet] are all but insuperable', and these works 'exhibit the carelessness of scoring which mars his incomparable gifts of melody'.

Stone's concluding remarks on the clarinet's weak points carry a particular resonance even today, concentrating on two areas which are still regarded as problematic.

> [The clarinet] is singularly susceptible to atmospheric changes, and rises in pitch very considerably, indeed more than any other instrument, with warmth. It is therefore essential, after playing for some time, to flatten the instrument; a caution often neglected. On the other hand it does not bear large alterations of pitch without becoming out of tune. In this respect it is the most difficult of all the orchestral instruments, and for this reason it ought undoubtedly to exercise the privilege now granted by ancient usage to the oboe; that, namely of giving the pitch to the band . . . Lastly, the whole beauty of the instrument depends on the management of the reed. A player, however able, is very much at the mercy of this part of the mechanism. A bad reed not only takes all quality away, but exposes its possessor to the horrible shriek termed *couac* (i.e. 'quack') by the French, and a 'goose' in the vernacular. There is no instrument in which failure of lip or deranged keys produce so unmusical a result, or one so impossible to conceal; and proportionate care should be exercised in its prevention.

The late nineteenth century

Other contemporary perceptions of the clarinet can be deduced from the orchestration treatises by Berlioz's successors in the field, including Gevaert and Rimsky-Korsakov. Writing in Hamburg in mid-century, Robert

Vollstedt reported, 'The clarinet is not only the finest wind instrument in the orchestra, but also the one with the widest range. The sound of the clarinet is closest to the human voice. What a wealth of resources composers have here to achieve the finest effects.'[30] Carl Baermann also remarked that the clarinet's close similarity to a fine singing voice enabled the performer to speak to the heart:

> The finer the tone, the more poetic the effect. The tone is fine when it has a full, vibrant, metallic sound, and retains the same characteristics at all volumes and in all registers, when the tone does not deteriorate at full strength, and does not leave a piercing impression; when it is so expressive and flexible that it can perform all the notes lightly and smoothly in the quiet passages – in a word, when it resembles a superlatively fine and full soprano voice. If this register (the best on the clarinet) is fine-toned, then the lower notes will of themselves also be so, and one is on the right track. But even if the tone possesses all those characteristics and lacks inner life – the 'divine spark' intrinsic to man as a guarantee of his destiny, 'the soul' – then all effort and striving is of no avail, for this frigid music cannot be touched by the fire of Prometheus.[31]

Gevaert echoed this appreciation of the clarinet's versatility, 'so long as fluent passages are not too far removed from its most usual keys'.[32] Documentation of the period around 1900 is well served by Richard Strauss's revision of Berlioz, as well as by Cecil Forsyth's treatise.[33] Oscar Street's article already cited gives an excellent idea of the clarinet's overall status in England in 1916, reckoning that Mühlfeld's tone and execution left something to be desired and deploring the prevalent habit of glorifying foreigners.

Matters of style are especially well addressed in violin tutors from various parts of the century, including Spohr (Vienna, 1832), Baillot (Paris, 1834) and Joachim and Moser (Berlin, 1902–5), the last of these particularly applicable to Brahms interpretation. Like many of his contemporaries, Brahms notated legato by means of a series of smaller-scale slurs, whose intent and meaning in various contexts remained ambiguous throughout the nineteenth century. There was no longer the eighteenth-century expectation that the slur indicated an expressive accent followed by diminuendo, in every context; such characteristics might well be contradicted by the musical sense. Brymer draws an analogy between Brahms's phrasing and string bowing, proposing between slurs 'just a gentle brush of the tongue . . . or no sort of tongue-action at all, if it is felt that this is more natural'.[34] But even with legato passages it seems probable that today's clarinettists employ a smaller range of articulations than Mühlfeld, with nuance determined less evidently by the harmony. Indeed, his performances were given at a time when musical tempo was considerably more flexible than it is today, and fluctuations in the surface rhythm of individual passages as well as in basic pulse for longer sections were common.

Early recordings and musical style

Early recordings have recently become recognised as invaluable primary evidence. They illustrate an approach to the clarinet (and other instruments) which places a high premium on characterisation rather than the extreme clarity and accuracy within strict tempo which nowadays tends to be taken for granted.[35] An essential guide to the whole subject is Robert Philip's *Early Recordings and Musical Style* (Cambridge, 1992). Before 1900 a generally more spontaneous approach to performance was the norm. To consider that orchestral performances at the turn of the century were under-rehearsed, and therefore of a low standard, is to judge them from our own perspective. In relation to rhythm, 'it is impossible to draw a clear distinction between competence and style. A rhythm which now sounds unclear or slapdash would be judged unclear or under-rehearsed by the modern listener, but would not necessarily have seemed so to an early twentieth-century audience.' Indeed, even such a basic matter as tempo flexibility can scarcely be deduced from composers' own comments which take for granted the musical taste of *their* times, not ours. As Philip notes, we would be unable to deduce from notated scores the degree of flexibility of Elgar's tempos, the prominence of Joachim's portamento, the lightness of rhythm of Bartók's piano playing, the reedy tone of French bassoons and clarinets in Stravinsky's Paris recordings, or the nature of Rakhmaninov's rubato. According to a colleague, Joachim had an unpredictable approach to tempo: 'to play with him is damned difficult. Always different tempi, different accents.'[36]

One of Philip's most important conclusions is that changes in tone-quality over the twentieth century pale into insignificance compared with other changes in performance practice. Even within this general thesis he suggests that the history of clarinet-playing in the early twentieth century is much simpler than that of oboe- or flute-playing. Whilst the French and German schools of playing remained strongly differentiated in tone quality, vibrato is hardly ever mentioned by writers on the clarinet. In 1931 F. G. Rendall stated that a sustained vibrato 'is quite impossible on the clarinet',[37] though it was his compatriots Reginald Kell, Jack Brymer and Gervase de Peyer (amongst others) who were to prove otherwise. Unlike the flute and oboe, the clarinet was played without vibrato in America as late as the 1940s, its only tonal development during the preceding two decades being a tendency towards a greater dynamic range and sometimes an increase in detailed nuancing. How far back in history can these traits of early recordings be traced? Perhaps not just Brahms but Mozart premières were more spontaneous than any interpretation today on period or modern instruments. Inevitably, earlier techniques and conventions can never be totally recaptured, but their very investigation has the capacity to enhance our lives both as musicians and clarinettists.

3 Equipment

Aspects of standardisation

Before purchasing an early clarinet, a player should ideally acquire some working knowledge of original instruments and manufacturers, since the choice of clarinet needs to be based on a combination of practical and historical considerations. National differences in manufacture are especially important.[1] A major inventory of instrument collections world-wide is Phillip T. Young's *4900 Historical Woodwind Instruments*, whilst *The New Langwill Index* by William Waterhouse is an indispensable reference source. Nowadays, students routinely debate at length the merits of the many Boehm-system clarinets currently on the market. Yet for all their slight structural differences these instruments are far more standardised and uniform than their counterparts in previous times.

Pitch has been unrealistically standardised in recent historical performance, with an almost exclusive focus upon $a' = 415$ (baroque), $a' = 430$ (classical) and $a' = 435$ or 440 (Romantic).[2] This is no more than a convenient and over-simplified response to the evidence, even though the degree of acceptable compromise must clearly vary according to musical context. But for ensemble playing today's historical pitches have become so widely accepted that they cannot be ignored when purchasing either copies or original clarinets. Ironically, Quantz lamented the lack of a uniform pitch, which he reckoned was inconvenient to his work as a flautist and detrimental to music in general; he expressed the hope that a universal standard would soon find favour. Significantly, an advertisement in the *Wiener Zeitung* of 25 February 1789 contained a request from the woodwind maker Friedrich Lempp that prospective foreign clients should specify the required pitch, 'whether Vienna pitch, *Kammerton*, or even French pitch, or send him a tuning fork . . .'[3]

Classical clarinets

The age of Mozart is an obvious starting point for the period clarinettist. English clarinets survive in by far the greatest numbers, but in some respects they are quite distinct from continental counterparts, for example in their relatively high pitch of around a′ = 440. In his survey of eighteenth-century clarinets in European collections, David Ross found many more English clarinets for examination than from all other European countries combined. The five- (and six-) keyed clarinet had an extraordinarily long time-span of service; many English specimens are nineteenth-century instruments probably used by bandsmen and amateur players rather than in the concert hall.[4] It seems that this was the market for which the many instruction books were published, and the relatively high pitch (together with the scarcity of A clarinets) might support the theory of military band usage. Characteristic features are their long-tenon mouthpiece and a 'waisted' barrel shape, quite unlike continental models. Furthermore, when a sixth key is present, it is a long Rl trill key for a′/b′, rather than the L4 c♯′/g♯″ usually found elsewhere. David Ross observed that the relatively small amount of undercutting contributed to the lighter timbre of English clarinets, and in *The New Grove* Nicholas Shackleton remarked that English instruments of the late eighteenth century were probably tonally similar to continental instruments of two or more decades earlier.

By contrast, the Bohemian clarinet of Mozart's time had already evolved somewhat further than in other countries. Its larger tone-holes, especially at the lower end of the instrument, led to a fuller tone in the chalumeau register which was famously exploited by Mozart. Surviving Viennese classical clarinets are unfortunately rare, though there are examples by Theodor Lotz and Kaspar Tauber, amongst others. The Lotz B♭ clarinet in Geneva's Musée des Instruments Anciens de Musique was examined in detail by David Ross. Lotz was royal and imperial court instrument maker in Vienna, and remains of immense importance as the maker of Stadler's clarinets. Amongst various advanced features (given that Lotz died in 1792) are the division of the barrel from mouthpiece and stock from bell, making a total of six sections; there are some particularly extravagant ivory mountings. Both long keys are secured with metal saddles in order to reduce sideways play, a feature found only later elsewhere; furthermore, the a♭/e♭″ R4 key is arched back towards the f/c″ hole, alleviating this rather difficult slide. Ross reckoned that the instrument possessed the largest, thickest sound of any eighteenth-century specimens he tested, rounded and woody throughout its entire range, in the tradition of the best German players (and instruments) of today. Particularly impressive were the good intonation between the registers and the evenness of scale in the lower register. He suggested that the dynamic range and timbral quality of this Lotz clarinet are no doubt related to the very large bore size (between 15.00 and 15.05 mm) found on the instrument. We are indeed fortunate that this Lotz clarinet survives in such excellent condition, since much of the organological evidence is less directly focussed. As has recently been observed, 'many Viennese clarinets from the time of Mozart and Beethoven were in use for most of the nineteenth century with new keys added, broken keys removed and the holes blocked up, cracks glued, new mouthpieces added, as they were used successively in orchestras, town bands, dance bands and bars'.[5]

In France there is little documentation of clarinet making before the 1780s, though after the Revolution the situation changed radically with the foundation of the Paris Conservatoire, the subsequent appearance of Lefèvre's tutor and the manufacture of clarinets by makers of the stature of Simiot in Lyons. As we remarked in Chapter 1, an almost universal custom in continental Europe was the use of alternative middle joints (*pièces de rechange*) for B♭ and A clarinets. This was a convenient compromise because the most expensive piece of the instrument was the lowest part, with thicker wood (for the bell) and three keys. The practice of using *pièces de rechange* has become very popular amongst today's period players, and operates much more satisfactorily in orchestral music than one has any right to expect. Both orchestral and chamber repertories also demand the C clarinet in the tonalities of F major and C major, for technical as well as colouristic reasons; the key of D is especially difficult to negotiate on the classical B♭ clarinet and was frequently warned against in tutors. Indeed, Mozart advised his pupil Thomas Attwood to notate parts for the clarinet only in F and C, though in his own works he was somewhat more enterprising.

The configuration of the widely played five-keyed clarinet was supplemented by a sixth key as early as 1768,[6] and by 1802 Lefèvre's tutor enthusiastically recommended a key for c♯′, which he said was otherwise indistinguishable from the semitone above! Though this sixth key is absent from the clarinets illustrating both his diatonic and chromatic fingering charts, it is present in his sketch of the component parts of the clarinet.[7] In the same year that Lefèvre was writing, the double-hole sometimes provided as an alternative was regarded in Koch's *Lexicon* as essential to avoid a dull and poorly tuned note. By 1808 an anonymous writer in the *Allgemeine musikalische Zeitung* was recommending at least nine keys to avoid scarcely usable chalumeau notes, citing Mozart's Concerto as evidence and addressing fears of malfunction by stating that his own new clarinet had been played daily for nine months without needing a single repair.

An eight-keyed clarinet will play fluently in all the tonalities commonly used by composers of the period up to 1830, and there remains a dilemma for what repertory to add these two or three extra keys to the classic five-key design; overall, today's continental players have been less inclined to do so than the British or Americans. The provision of extra keys needs to be weighed against the characteristic veiled tone-quality produced by cross-fingerings, which can contribute a great deal to the musical expression. Mechanism was originally added to instruments principally to facilitate trills, but it also had the effect of making woodwinds more powerful in sound, sometimes at the expense of variety of tonal character. Heinrich Grenser was strikingly nonchalant about extra keys, writing in 1800: 'To add a key in order to improve this note or that is neither difficult nor artful. And then keys are not all that new, for when I was a boy I made use of them in order to bolster up the weak notes, and it became easy to give them their proper place.'[8] We should remember that all the great makers, including Simiot and the Grensers, manufactured clarinets with a wide variety of key configurations. At least as important as the mechanism, of course, is the question of matching tone-quality to appropriate repertory. An early nine-teenth-century clarinet will probably not be idiomatic for Mozart's music.

Nineteenth-century clarinets

The advance of the historical performance movement beyond Beethoven to Berlioz, Mendelssohn, Schumann, Brahms and even Verdi has been the inspiration for practical investigation of various designs of nine-teenth-century clarinet already familiar from history books. As we have already observed, most of these instruments owe a considerable debt to the thirteen-keyed model developed by Iwan Müller. Less important than Müller's actual mechanism was the way in which his keys were constructed, disposed, vented and padded. He replaced the flat leather pad with wool-filled leather pads held in a hollow cup which was angled to allow adequate venting. Holes were countersunk to present a raised, bevelled ring to the pad, a feature nowadays familiar from the modern instrument. Among Müller's additional achievements was his promotion of the metal ligature, and a thinner, more tapered reed, enabling a wider range of articulation. The keys were arranged to give the best possible acoustic result, and to allow performance in a variety of tonalities. Several writers, including Kroll and Weston, have given a detailed account of his new mechanism, which in addition to Lefèvre's six keys comprised: an open-standing key to close a re-positioned f/c″ hole; a cross-key for R3, giving b♭/f″; a long b/f♯″ key for R5; an e♭'/b♭″ cross-key for L3; an f'/c‴ key for L2; a g♯' key for L1 (as Boehm); a long a'/b' trill-key for R1. Müller also provided alternative right-hand thumb touch pieces to the a♭/e♭″ and f♯/c♯″ keys.

As we have observed, the Müller clarinet was developed by Carl Baermann *c.* 1860 by the addition of extensions to keys so that they could be played by different fingers, and by duplication of keys so that fingers of the opposite hand could be used; to Müller's thirteen keys were added a further five or seven. In England the Albert-system thirteen-keyed clarinet was truly overtaken in popularity by the Boehm only in the 1930s, as composers' technical demands became ever increasing. Even in *The Oxford Companion to Music*, first published in 1938, the Albert system is illustrated as the normal clarinet and some twenty years later it was still being played in at least one major British orchestra. Conversely, the Boehm had begun to take root as early as the 1880s, when the virtuoso Henry Lazarus wrote his *Method* for both systems (though he did not himself change to the Boehm), and the Spanish Gomez brothers arrived in England, having been taught the Boehm clarinet by Klosé's pupil Rose.

Although nineteenth-century clarinets are still relatively available, their pitch level can be a serious difficulty. In particular, Old Philharmonic Pitch was the norm in Victorian England, and at a' = 452 lay approximately a semitone above our modern standard. Since it was in use until the 1920s, there are still many surviving instruments at high pitch which are not necessarily marked as such (although lower, i.e. 'modern' pitched clarinets may carry the stamped indication 'LP'). In a useful survey of earlier twentieth-century pitches, Anthony Baines also draws attention to the Continental or French Pitch of a' = 435, at which many clarinets were built and which Joachim in his violin treatise of 1902–5 implies is standard pitch. However, German pitch was sometimes higher, as shown by the pitch of a' = 440 of Mühlfeld's surviving clarinets.

Rendall's description of the key-systems and tone-quality of nineteenth-century clarinets makes essential reading, particularly when supplemented by Baines's various fingering charts. Rendall addresses the crucial question of whether there is indeed a difference in tone between Boehm- and Müller-type clarinets, suggesting that there is certainly less than between French and German bassoons; some hypersensitive ears might detect a more open tone in the Boehm, and a more veiled tone in the Müller, due to its forked fingerings and greater number of closed holes. He admits that it is now recognised that on average there is some difference between the characteristic tones of the Müller and Boehm types, which by scientific analysis can be traced to the configuration of the bore and the disposition and treatment of the holes; clearly, the difference in styles and schools of playing must also be taken into account. Kroll's book offers an interesting German perspective, attributing native objection to the Boehm on the grounds of timbre, which he claims is brighter, thinner, whilst smoother and more uniform. On the whole German clarinettists (he says) prefer the slightly less homogeneous but darker, rounder sound of German clarinets. An important distinction exists between the wide mouthpiece of the Boehm with its relatively open lay and light, wide reed, and the closer German lay and heavy, narrow reed.

Many nineteenth-century clarinets respond in quite different ways from the Boehm system. Whatever the advantages of thirteen-keyed systems (for example, a greater freedom at the top of the clarinet register around c'''), sheer mobility in extreme tonalities is unlikely to match the Boehm, even on a clarinet whose keywork ensures clarity over the entire chromatic compass. In terms of tone quality, nationality of clarinet can be a more important element than the detail of keywork. Nineteenth-century repertory as a whole dictates an interest in German clarinets; as we have noted, Hermstedt had already constructed something similar to Müller's design for the Spohr concertos, whilst Heinrich Baermann graduated via ten keys to a twelve-keyed instrument for Weber's solo works. Fig. 3.1 shows the latter instrument with fingering chart, as depicted by Vanderhagen in 1819. The illustration indicates that Baermann made use of a special extending barrel.

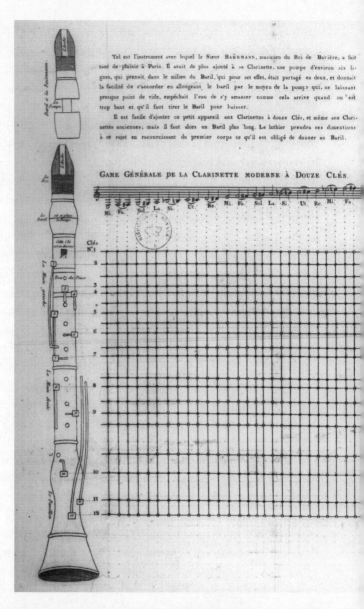

Fig. 3.1 Fingering chart for Heinrich Baermann's twelve-keyed clarinet,
from Amand Vanderhagen's *Nouvelle méthode pour la clarinette
moderne à douze clés* (Paris, 1819)

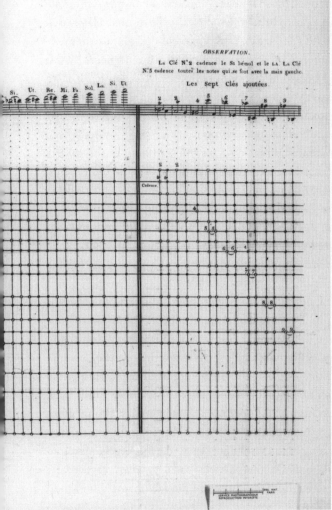

Thirteen-keyed French clarinets in C, B♭ and (more rarely) A have survived in some numbers. Berlioz's treatise welcomed the increased sophistication of mechanism, remarking that 'the manufacture of these instruments, which remained for so long in its infancy, is nowadays in a state of progress which cannot fail to bring the most valuable results'. He praised the greater compass, facility and legato of Sax's recent designs, also approving the use of metal rather than wood as material for mouthpieces. It was surely a thirteen-keyed boxwood clarinet of which Berlioz wrote: 'It is an *epic* instrument . . . whose voice is that of heroic love . . .' Such a comment demands that the rich tonal palette of these clarinets be investigated. Baines (p. 332) noted that 'individual artistry apart, these old thirteen-keyed boxwood clarinets are almost unbeatable for tone, so long as the correct mouthpiece and small, hard reed are used with them'. The fine intonation and tone of the large-bore Alberts were recognised by Rendall – 'they have in fact never been surpassed' – and were, generally speaking, much superior to the contemporary Boehm. Only the increasing technical demands of composers persuaded players to change to the Boehm. Baines quotes Bernard Shaw's celebrated comparison of English and German players during the later career of Lazarus in the 1890s: the Germans 'use reeds which give a more strident, powerful, appealing tone than in England; and the result is that certain passages (in *Der Freischütz,* for example) come out with a passion and urgency that surprises the tourist used to Egerton, Lazarus and Clinton. But in the *Parsifal* Prelude, or the second movement of Beethoven's Fourth Symphony, one misses the fine tone and dignified continence of the English fashion.'[9] Baines noted that this comparison continued much later, after the widespread adoption of the Boehm clarinet in England. It has often been argued that the greater technical fluency of the Boehm was achieved only at the expense of some of the resonance which the relatively uncovered bore of the Albert allowed. Original Ottensteiner clarinets as used by Mühlfeld are less easy to acquire and thus have already inspired boxwood copies.

How essential is a C clarinet for this period? During the nineteenth century it maintained an important role, especially in Italy and in Eastern Europe. Verdi followed Rossini in scoring for it on a regular basis, whilst Smetana in *The Bartered Bride* variously specifies C and B♭ clarinets in contexts which in earlier times would have been the exclusive province of the C clarinet. As for the mainstream German tradition, Schubert retained the C clarinet in his Ninth Symphony, but Mendelssohn heralded its withdrawal in preferring A clarinets in that key, with a signature of three flats. There were then only occasional appearances before its revival by Mahler and Strauss, for example in the scherzo of Brahms's Fourth Symphony. In chamber music, Schubert's Octet requires a C clarinet in the Variation movement, whilst Spohr's *Notturno* for wind band and Turkish instruments also has a prominent part. But notwithstanding such exceptional pieces as the *Schottische Bilder* by Loewe, the C clarinet went into a sharp decline as a solo instrument, as mechanism enabled a wider variety of tonalities to be played on the Bb. Many writers including Berlioz (himself a champion of the C clarinet) and the players Berr and Baermann emphasise that the choice of clarinet should always be the responsibility of the composer, not the player. For this reason, the writer and theorist Gottfried Weber in 1829 preferred clarinet parts transposed in the score, rather than the French custom of writing parts at pitch, which left too much choice for the player.

Original instruments

The most likely sources for acquiring an original instrument tend to be auction houses and dealers. Some idea of auction prices can be gleaned from *Early Music*, whose columns report regularly on sales and their catalogues. Old instruments survive in a variety of condition; the finest are still eminently playable, but internal bore measurements are especially susceptible to change, and there may also be evidence of attempts to alter the pitch. Early clarinets are sometimes not in playing condition for minor reasons (such as leaking pads), though even small structural damage may detract from an instrument's value. Furthermore, a clarinet's musical potential may be evident only after some months' playing. Dealers have the contacts to discover instruments which the individual might not otherwise encounter, though it is still true that interesting old clarinets continue to surface in some unlikely places. Antiques have a special value for the amount of historical information they can impart; whereas clarinets by the very best makers tend to inspire replicas, there are sometimes originals for sale by lesser-known manufacturers which turn out well. An original clarinet may also have an investment value with which a copy can never compete, simply because of the laws of supply and demand. It should be added here that antiques can be particularly prone to cracking when subjected to the changes in atmospheric conditions associated with central heating or air travel; curators of collections worldwide vary widely in their attitude to conservation, some allowing instruments to be borrowed, others promoting policies closer to a museum culture.

Copies

Naturally, clarinettists of the past played new instruments, and this in itself might be thought sufficient justification for using a replica, rather than searching for an original (Fig. 3. 2).[10] The opportunity to commission a copy of a specific historical clarinet is a relatively recent development, and nowadays some of the best but rare French, German and Austrian instruments are being recreated by makers of various nationalities. Thus the player is in a position to choose both make and model. Surveys of clarinet makers have rarely been attempted and are in any case liable to become quickly out of date in an ever-changing market-place. But one such account dating from 1996–7 found a huge range of models available from some nine manufacturers, including such specialised projects as early bass clarinets and *clarinettes d'amour*.[11]

What actually is a copy ? A realistic answer might be that it usually contains both old and new elements, though in a proportion not always fully comprehended by the player or colleagues.[12] One priority must be that any clarinet should respond well as a musical instrument. As John Solum has suggested in relation to the flute, the greatest antiques may have tonal superiorities to the best modern replicas, but the degree of difference is not as much as generally exists between old and new stringed instruments. A greater aesthetic danger is rather that relatively few historical clarinets are being copied in relation to the rapidly increasing number of players, implying a degree of standardisation which originally did not exist.

As the various designs of the Boehm clarinet readily prove, the tuning of any clarinet is something of a compromise, each of the twelfths having its own special problems, with bore size and undercutting of holes varying from one design to the next. Playing early clarinets inevitably involves the performer more closely in questions of tuning, and the extent to which the

Fig. 3.2 Copies of ten-keyed B♭ clarinet *c.* 1810 by Heinrich Grenser (Daniel Bangham, 1991) and two-keyed D clarinet *c.* 1710 by Jacob Denner (Brian Ackerman, 1983), together with Boehm-system clarinet

solutions of the original maker are to be followed should be an important initial decision. The use of an electronic tuner to impose equal temperament can be misguided in purely historical terms. Backofen noted that he had never encountered a clarinet with absolutely pure intonation and that he could not decide whether this was inherent in the instrument or the fault of makers. He warns against clarinets whose registers are not in tune, and Fröhlich endorses this piece of excellent advice. Once a clarinet has been made, individual notes may be flattened by filling the next open hole, emphasising the lower (undercut) part of the hole to affect the fundamental register. Wax was originally used, though for slight adjustments opaque nail polish is a useful (and easily removable) modern alternative. As Backofen's tutor remarks, embouchure has an important part to play (and this is especially true of boxwood instruments), together with liberal use of alternative fingerings. It is worth noting that he placed a very high priority on accurate intonation. Players in Mozart's day tended to be suspicious of extra keywork, because it seemed to add to technical difficulties, and it also carried an increased risk of leaking pads. Backofen remarked that half-broken springs were all too common.

Particular problems are associated with different types of early clarinets, though it is clearly essential at the outset to establish the intended pitch level. For example, on the soprano chalumeau it is especially important to tune the cross-fingerings so that the instrument will play chromatically with accurate intonation. The higher part of the compass must be stable and controllable. No more than one or two notes in the upper register are demanded of any of the sizes of chalumeau, and so the normal challenge on clarinets of voicing the twelfths does not really apply. Cross-fingerings on the larger sizes also need to be carefully tuned. The dimensions and design of the mouthpiece have a radical effect on tone-quality and some makers have opted for synthetic materials with palpable success.

In playing the baroque clarinet, one needs to keep in mind Nicholas Shackleton's observation that 'the assumption that one can use identical fingering in the chalumeau and clarinet registers has rather less validity on earlier clarinets than modern ones'.[13] On copies of Jacob Denner (for Handel and Vivaldi) and Zencker (for Molter) the clarinet's focus is its upper register; lower notes will need humouring – which usually means flattening. As with all clarinets, baroque instruments need constant playing before their true potential can be revealed, since apparent limitations in a particular clarinet may well turn out to be the responsibility of the performer.

On classical instruments the exquisite chromatic scale obtained with cross-fingerings is smoothed out when extra keys are added to the five which are sufficient for Mozart's chamber and orchestral music. Some old instruments are furnished with a L3 double hole for c♯' and this feature can also be used for R1 to obtain b in the chalumeau register. On later ten-keyed models with a b♭/f″ cross-key for R3, the relevant hole can be tuned to favour the low register, with cross-fingering used in the clarinet register. Each of the principal nineteenth-century models has its own particular characteristics and challenges. An instrument such as the Baermann-system clarinet demands well-made and regulated keywork. A boxwood clarinet carrying this degree of mechanism needs to be made of well-seasoned material if it is to give lasting service. Naturally, the keys on any wind instrument need to be functioning properly and the pads forming an effective seal. Experience will indicate the amount of playing that is advisable before a clarinet revisits the manufacturer for further adjustment.

Mouthpieces

Mouthpieces of all types can now be copied with a greater degree of accuracy than in the past. Opinions vary as to what material should be used; from an historical point of view, it is generally true that once the idea of separating mouthpiece and barrel had been established, boxwood mouthpieces were replaced by harder materials. Ivory, glass and metal were alternatives, with ebonite eventually introduced towards the end of the nineteenth century. A wooden mouthpiece always carries the risk of warping, and some of today's historical players have opted for ebonite, believing any change of tone-quality to be scarcely discernible and easily outweighed by its superior stability. There is a broader philosophical point here about the extent to which developments in manufacture should generally be taken on board. In fact, many of today's makers offer a compromise multi-purpose 'early' mouthpiece, often designed with a full-length table down to the base, allowing the use of a commercial (often German-cut) reed. The superficial advantages of such a package should not preclude further individual research. In fact, the dimensions of clarinet mouthpieces have been subject to considerable change. The very earliest clarinets have disproportionately broad mouthpieces, but from the middle of the eighteenth century they were considerably narrower than they are today. On classical clarinets built around 1800 the mouthpieces were broadest in England and northern Germany, and narrowest in France (where they became broader from the early nineteenth century) and in Austria and adjoining areas (where very narrow mouthpieces survived longest). It is rather surprising that Viennese instruments, which were designed to generate a good tone in the chalumeau register, did so with such a narrow mouthpiece. As a general rule, the lay on earlier mouthpieces was relatively long and the tip opening relatively narrow, so that it resembled the modern German lay more closely than that associated with Boehm-system clarinets.

Reeds

It may come as something of a relief to learn that, even in the eighteenth century, clarinettists had reason to complain about their reeds. Both Vanderhagen and Baermann lamented the poor quality of available cane. An important difference between the habits of eighteenth- and nineteenth-century clarinettists and players today concerns the manufacture of the reed. Although ready-made reeds have been available for sale since the late eighteenth century, their use by the majority of clarinettists is largely a twentieth-century phenomenon. Since aspiring clarinettists needed to be able to make reeds for their own use almost immediately they began playing the instrument, many early tutors contain useful instructions, including the selection of cane and reed adjustment.

One of the earliest commentators on the subject of reeds was Vanderhagen. He advised beginners to choose a reed neither too hard nor too soft.[14] Regarding the choice of cane, Vanderhagen warns against that which is too spongy. He suggests that the player select dryish cane with pores neither too large nor too small. His more specific instructions concerning the actual manufacturing process imply that once the reed was finished, it was then subjected to considerable fine-tuning for days afterwards. Vanderhagen's *Méthode nouvelle* was extremely popular throughout Europe for at least three decades after it was published. The anonymous *Metodo facilissimo*, largely a reprint of Vanderhagen, adds to the latter's instructions that, only by repeating the process of reed-making can the best experience be gained.[15]

Lefèvre offers the following advice: anything too soft produces a disagreeable sound; especially when articulated, and does not have the consistency to 'spin' (*filer*) the sound; a reed that is too hard tires the chest, injures the lips, ruins the embouchure, makes the sound uneven, and allows air to escape, resulting in a smaller column of air through the instrument. Lefèvre instructs his pupil to leave enough wood when shaping a reed to give good high notes, and then to shorten the tip to give enough keenness to the chalumeau register. He remarks that it is rare to find good cane, since it is cut too green or too dry. When green it is spongy and produces a dull sound, whereas dry it lacks the sap to produce the necessary vibrations.

According to Backofen, all clarinettists should prepare their own reeds; he advises always having a spare in case of emergency. He prescribes no general rules for reed preparation, claiming that whilst one player may prefer harder reeds and be able to play them without straining, another player will opt for lighter reeds. Backofen stresses the importance of obtaining hard cane, which is brownish-gold in appearance and has an ivory colour when cut across. Whilst Backofen illustrates two ways of finishing the tip of the reed, he expresses a preference for that which renders it thinnest at the tip.[16] He also recommends scraping notches into the surface of the reed to assist its tying onto the mouthpiece.[17] Amongst the tools needed to make reeds, Backofen suggests a piece of wood with an indentation cut into it, a sharp knife, a large wide file and a small piece of glass or a piece of horsetail (*Equisetum arvense*) dipped in water.

Fröhlich offers the most extensive commentary on the selection and construction of the reed.[18] It is important to ensure that the back of the reed is flat, and the reed must be kept clean by removing saliva from it after playing. Fröhlich provides explicit instructions on how to transform a circular piece of cane into a reed, and confirms earlier writers' preferences for a particular quality of cane. He suggests that when the reed weakens at the tip, its life can be prolonged by trimming it and moving it towards the tip of the mouthpiece. In the case of new reeds, Fröhlich recommends that after they are tied onto the mouthpiece, both the new reed and the mouthpiece should be soaked in water for approximately five minutes![19] As well as those tools of reed-making mentioned above, Fröhlich mentions the use of Dutch rush for filing reeds. He too advises the player to remove all moisture from the reed after playing. Carl Baermann favours the combination of both a good reed and a good mouthpiece. He remarks that, despite efforts to find a better material for the reed, cane remains a necessary evil. It seems that Baermann usually prepared between six and twelve reeds at a time, and after playing a new reed for a day or two, he rubbed the flat surface with sandstone to preserve its smoothness.

Care and maintenance

Given that the keywork of an early clarinet is fully operational, maintenance consists largely of taking special care of the wood. Boxwood instruments are especially susceptible to changes in atmospheric conditions, and particular care needs to be taken when playing in cold temperatures, since the difference in temperature between a warm interior of the bore and a cold exterior can cause splits and cracks. The oiling of modern clarinets is still controversial, but is essential for boxwood. Ted Planas has pointed out the difference between the dense texture of blackwood, the progressively less dense woods of palisander, rosewood, tulip wood and cocus, and the relative lightness of boxwood.[20] Entirely comprised of sapwood, the fresh living part of the tree-trunk directly beneath the bark, boxwood is capable of carrying moisture through its grain more easily than the heartwoods at the centre of the trunk. Oiling with boiled or raw linseed, or with Backofen's recommended almond oil (better for the inside of the bore), produces a varnish and helps to reduce the absorption of water when rubbed in well with the excess shaken off. Unlike the blackwoods, boxwood is very good at absorbing water and, as the nineteenth-century maker Mahillon remarked, is more suitable as a hygrometer than as a musical instrument! Incidentally, leather pads soon harden and lose their effectiveness if allowed to come into contact with the oil.

Detailed advice on instrument maintenance (and reeds) is contained within the 'Musick Plan' by Mozart's clarinettist, Anton Stadler, and may usefully be cited here:

> Of the woodwind instruments one must also add that the masters should know how to make the very necessary and customary reeds themselves and as soon as possible should instruct their pupils to

make good reeds, because a performer will seldom progress very
far on his instrument if he cannot make reeds himself and repair
his instrument with his own hand, that is *leather* and also *feather*,
for which the necessary tools, such as good carving-knives, small
knives, files, screwdrivers, grindstone, small tongs, sealing wax,
leather, string, and the like are necessary; also woodwind instruments should be cleaned frequently and well oiled because they
[then] respond more easily (especially in the summer) and at the
same time must be guarded against early deterioration. Because, if
a wind instrument is not always in proper condition, so that all
parts (pins, pegs) are well wrapped, all key-covers secure, and the
reed responding correctly, then the player cannot feel sure [of
himself], his tone is uncertain, the bass [notes] whistle, and the
high notes scream, so that even if the artist has a great deal of
talent, taste, and good delivery, his tone will nevertheless be bad,
and to the ear of the attentive music lover and of the connoisseur
[he] will be just as disagreeable as a composition attractively and
artistically styled, learned and completely engraved, which has
then been scrawled with poor ink on coarse paper with a miserable
pen, is to the reader accustomed to [elegant] calligraphy.[21]

Both Backofen and Fröhlich advise checking the keywork as a first priority. Fröhlich adds that if a key is not sealing it should be examined to see if it
has become bent. Most writers warn that leaking pads can produce faulty
intonation and should be replaced. Fröhlich describes the practice, still in
use today, whereby the tone-holes and lower end of each joint are covered
whilst the player sucks the remaining air from the enclosed joint, to ensure
that the pads are forming a correct seal. The tone-holes must also be cleaned
especially if they have accumulated dirt, removable by blowing the hole with
the mouth. One source warns that unless done with care, this may impare
the intonation, confirming that many players inserted material into the
tone-holes of their instrument with tuning in mind.[22] The tenons should
always be wound with enough thread to ensure that they fit together com-
fortably. Fröhlich recommends the use of strong waxed thread and provides
detailed instructions on how best to wind it around the tenon. He adds that
weak springs may cause pad leakage and that their strength should be

sufficient to ensure that the pad covers the hole with ease. Backofen notes that often springs are already in need of repair before one checks them.

Whilst one source recommends that the whole instrument (without the keys) be washed clean with pure water and then swabbed out after playing, the majority of writers advise the use of a pull-through to rid the instrument of remaining moisture. Backofen instructs the player to pull-through each individual part of the clarinet and to keep the instrument vertical to allow moisture to evaporate. Fröhlich expresses a preference for a silk swab and recommends storing the instrument in a case to protect it from dust.

Amongst the more general aspects of clarinet maintenance which are mentioned in early source materials are hints to keep the clarinet away from warmth, such as sunshine, or a stove or heater. One writer advised that humidity had a detrimental effect on the wood, causing it to warp and crack. Players were warned against putting a damp clarinet away as this increased the likelihood of damaging the pads through their absorption of moisture. In addition, Fröhlich wisely instructed the player to exercise caution with the tube of the speaker key.

4   Playing historical clarinets

BY INGRID PEARSON

Introduction

The clarinet underwent a remarkable transformation during the
century which separated the publication of Carl Baermann's *Vollständige
Clarinett-Schule* from Roeser's *Essai d'instruction* of 1764. Indeed, the
instrument moved from the periphery of art music to a position of pre-
eminence amongst the orchestral winds. This chapter examines the principal primary sources for playing technique, with particular emphasis on
methods currently available in facsimile or reprint, such as those by Roeser,
Vanderhagen, Lefèvre, Backofen, Fröhlich, Müller, Klosé and Baermann.
They contain advice on many issues, including posture, embouchure and
reed-position, articulation, fingering, reed selection and maintenance, care
of the instrument, ornamentation, and other practical and aesthetic consid-
eratons.

The sheer variety of approaches within these sources provides a stark contrast with the homogeneity and standardisation of our own age. It is essential to bear in mind that many tutors were written in answer to the
requirements of an assortment of musicians, including advanced players,
beginner clarinettists, musical novices, composers and multi-instrumental-
ists. Although these sources are useful and informative, we cannot afford to
allow ourselves to be too entranced or enslaved by their directions, hints,
rules and suggestions.

Posture

One of the earliest representations of a clarinettist is the engraving
by the Nuremberg artist Johann Christoph Weigel. The depiction, from a set
entitled *Musicalisches Theatrum, c.* 1722, portrays a fashionably smart man
in an elegant room, playing a two-keyed clarinet whilst standing astride on a
platform.[1] However important the illustration as a documentary source, it

presents little useful information as regards the appropriate posture to adopt when playing the baroque clarinet. In fact, most representations of the two-keyed clarinet until about 1760 provide a similarly insufficient amount of detail. Whilst Eisel's *Musicus Autodidaktos* (1738) instructed players to place their hands on the instrument with the left hand above the right, as on the oboe, the manner of holding the clarinet received scant attention until around 1780, when *The Clarinet Instructor* advised holding the instrument 'near the Centre of the Body, the Bell Part inclining downwards, with the left Hand upper-most and the right lowest'.[2] These instructions continued to appear in other English-language publications as late as 1840.[3]

Eisel's text confirms that the earliest clarinet players were doublers. For such musicians (usually oboists), a fingering chart was probably their only requirement. As we have noted already, during the eighteenth century the now almost universal reed-below embouchure co-existed with the practice of placing the reed under the upper lip. This must have had some effect on the player's posture. The title page of Vanderhagen's first clarinet tutor, *Méthode nouvelle et raisonnée* (Paris, c. 1785), claimed to offer 'a clear and succinct explanation' of the manner in which the clarinet is held. He advised at the outset that the head not be held too high as this would hinder the breathing; it must be held naturally and without affectation. Vanderhagen provided measurements for the placement of both elbows and the bell of the clarinet in relation to the body. He preferred the wrists slightly inclined, and counselled against raising the fingers too far from the instrument. These instructions were echoed by most other writers of tutors for the five-keyed clarinet, including Blasius in his *Nouvelle méthode* (Paris, 1796).

Lefèvre's *Méthode de clarinette* (Paris, 1802) was specially commissioned by the Paris Conservatoire and proved to be of such lasting relevance to the art of clarinet playing that it was still being reissued well into the twentieth century.[4] In addition to a written description of how to hold the clarinet, conforming with those of Vanderhagen and Blasius, Lefèvre provided an illustration of a player's head with mouthpiece inserted in the mouth and both hands placed upon a five-keyed clarinet. He wrote that holding the instrument too high affected the upper register because the embouchure was then formed incorrectly; similarly, if the instrument was held too low then the player would become tired, making the tone too concentrated or repressed. Lefèvre followed earlier sources in stressing that the clarinet was to be held naturally; fingers should be curved and close to the holes, allowing the first joint a perpendicular and hammer-like descent on to the holes. Lefèvre made an explicit connection between posture and intonation, as discussed below.

Backofen's *Anweisung zur Klarinette* (Leipzig, *c*. 1803) is one of the earliest tutors to include instructions for both clarinet and basset horn. Backofen again emphasises the need for a relaxed posture, with the left hand held closest to the body, instructing players to place their feet 'as if they were about to make a large leap'.[5] He continues that with the head held too far back the clarinettist appears 'cheeky and shameless', but when held too far forward, the posture of the head gives 'a shy and unpromising appearance'! A further useful tip is his suggestion of assembling the exchange joints 'out of line', with the upper joint a little more to the left.

The didactic value of Lefèvre's illustration (entitled *Manière de tenir la clarinette*), is confirmed by its inclusion in Joseph Fröhlich's *Vollständige theoretische-praktische Musikschule*.[6] Fröhlich's quite detailed coverage of those issues discussed by Lefèvre discloses his esteem for (and perhaps even reliance upon) the latter's work. Fröhlich warns against holding the clarinet too high, as this increases the likelihood of moisture collecting in the tone holes. In contrast to the practice of Lefèvre and the Parisian school, whereby the holes were hammered shut with a perpendicular fall of the finger, Fröhlich advocated a flat fall of the finger onto the holes, ensuring their complete closure. He claimed that this method meant that a secure attack of tone was still possible but with 'far more ease and security'.[7]

Iwan Müller's *Méthode pour la nouvelle clarinette et clarinette-alto* (Paris, *c*. 1821) was essentially designed to promote his newly invented thirteen-keyed instrument. Müller's illustration of appropriate posture affords only a view of the two hands covering upper and lower joints. With the advent of the thirteen-keyed clarinet arose the popularity of the thumb rest added to the back of the lower joint, to assist the player in supporting the instrument's extra keywork. Klosé's *Méthode* (Paris, 1843) sought to elucidate matters pertaining to what is now known as the Boehm-system clarinet, but in far more detail than Müller's. The exhibition of Klosé's instrument, less than twenty years after Lefèvre's retirement in 1824 from the Paris Conservatoire, bears witness to the clarinet's rapid organological development during the nineteenth century. Klosé provided both pictorial and verbal indications as to how to hold the clarinet. As well as depicting good posture, he illustrated what he considers a 'constrained and defective position'.[8] Klosé reiterated the need to be relaxed, but also suggested that players concentrate their weight on the left foot, placing the right leg slightly forward. It is most likely that his specification of weight distribution sought to assist the player in accommodating the extra weight of the new Boehm clarinet. Although this tutor is applicable to the modern Boehm-system instrument, it contains some informative divergences from current performing practices, especially in the areas of breathing, fingering, melodic intonation and ornamentation. Performers on the Baermann-system clarinet can refer to Carl Baermann's *Vollständige Clarinett-Schule* for much valuable information.[9] His remarks concerning posture reiterate those of previous writers with regards to the position of the head, torso and arms. In addition, Baermann makes specific recommendations for the placement of particular fingers in order to facilitate the effective use of certain keys.

Embouchure and reed-position

The history of clarinet embouchure still remains largely unknown despite the fact that most eighteenth- and nineteenth-century writers considered it the basis of the art of wind playing. One writer even ventured to describe it as not only the most important aspect of sound production, but the sound production itself.[10] Lefèvre placed great importance on the embouchure because purity of execution depended upon it. For other writers, the entire subject was more allied with aesthetics and matters of taste; Klosé regarded the embouchure as 'the interpreter of our sensations and musical ideas', with its two most desirable ingredients being 'delicacy of tone and lightness of tongue'.[11]

We can be certain that during the early development of the clarinet, players had two reed-positions from which to choose.[12] Although the reed-below embouchure has survived almost exclusively through to the present day, practitioners of historical clarinets can hardly ignore the evidence with regard to the alternative position of reed-above.[13] But those players wishing to embrace the latter technique will find little in the way of detailed information. Despite Backofen's apparent ambivalence concerning the issue of clarinet reed-position, his remarks concerning basset horn reed-position are quite explicit; those who played reed-below placed the basset horn on their right side, in a manner similar to that adopted by bassoonists; and those who used the other reed-position put their right foot forward, resting the bell on the thigh, supposedly the most secure position. Although Müller's preference for the reed-below embouchure arose from the need to operate keywork with the right thumb, he too was ambivalent about reed-position. He wrote that reed-position 'is only habit, for one can have a beautiful quality of tone and excellent articulation from either method'.[14]

Vanderhagen's counsel against taking in too much of the mouthpiece and his advice to maintain an air-tight seal around it (sentiments echoed by almost all later writers) are of course equally applicable to reed-below players. Relevant to each category of player is also his advice that pressure on the reed from the lip should be increased as one ascends the scale, and decreased upon descending. In fact, Baermann, for whom the reed-above embouchure was simply 'wrong', gave almost the same advice. Fröhlich confirmed the sentiments of Vanderhagen, adding that one should take more of the mouthpiece in their mouth 'almost to the thread', in ascending through the clarinet's range. Fröhlich's observations concerning the reed-above embouchure were most probably a result of his experience of the playing of Philipp Meissner, clarinettist to the Würzburg Court between 1777 and 1802.[15] His most extensive remarks concern the methods of articulation most suited to each reed-position. Whilst the reed-below technique was better for tongued articulation, Fröhlich recommended the opposite reed-position as more suited to chest articulation and better able to facilitate alternation between the different registers of the clarinet.

Evidence of a 'golden age' of reed-above playing can be found in nineteenth-century Italian tutors, particularly those by Neapolitan players. Clarinettists and teachers, including Ferdinando Sebastiani and Gaetano Labanchi, Sebastiani's successor at both the Teatro San Carlo and the Conservatorio di San Pietro a Majella, confirm the link between clarinet reed-position and articulation, already implied by Lefèvre and Fröhlich. Sebastiani claimed that by employing the reed-above embouchure, one increased the types of colourings of articulation 'which give the clarinet its beauty'[16] and Labanchi stated that this method allowed for a more precise staccato. In his own clarinet method, published in 1883, Ferdinando Busoni, father of the pianist/composer Ferruccio and one of the latest nineteenth-century advocates of the technique, remained convinced that the reed-above embouchure assisted in obtaining a mellow timbre, pure intonation,

Fig. 4.1 The correct way to hold the clarinet, from Ferdinando Sebastiani's
Metodo per clarinetto (Naples, 1855)

flexibility and delicacy of nuance. The implications of Busoni's espousal of
this embouchure and the performance of his son's works for clarinet have
only recently attracted attention.[17]

Just as reed-position was not standardised, surviving reed-above sources
provided divergent opinions regarding the use of throat, chest and tongued
articulation, and in the latter case, which notes to tongue. It appears that by
the middle of the nineteenth century, Italian players had discarded the use of
the chest and throat as a means of reed-above articulation.[18] Sebastiani's
remarks that the technique allows the stronger and more stable of the lips to
manage the reed were completely contradicted less than thirty years later by
Busoni, for whom the upper lip's inherent weakness but greater elasticity
make it more suitable to regulate the reed. Klosé regarded the use of the

reed-below embouchure as advantageous for three reasons: the tone was softer and more agreeable, the position of the tongue under the reed allowed it to articulate better, and the overall appearance of the player was more graceful, allowing for greater powers of execution with much less effort.

Although Lefèvre's text made no explicit mention of reed-position, he instructed the player to place the mouthpiece between the lips, which in turn cover the teeth. Like Vanderhagen, Lefèvre favoured the reed-above position, as is clear from the illustrations in his tutor. Fröhlich advocated the double-lip embouchure, regardless of reed-position. He advised the player to be aware of the methods of modifying the embouchure in order to render the different registers of the clarinet 'according to the character of this instrument and the expression of the composer's desires'.[19] Like Backofen, Müller included very little information about embouchure, though there is some evidence that he (and many German players) bit into the top of the mouthpiece in an effort to grip it with their teeth.[20]

By far the most sophisticated commentary on the single-lip embouchure was written by Carl Baermann, for whom that method is a necessary outcome of the demands on clarinettists in the orchestra and as soloists. So convinced was Baermann by the placement of the teeth on the top of the mouthpiece that he claimed double-lip players needed only fourteen days' practice to reform their embouchure. To protect the mouthpiece from wear and tear inflicted by the teeth, Baermann recommended using a little silver strip as a mouthpiece patch.[21] More unusually, Baermann recommended a special technique for the production of higher pitches. With a gradual 'light turning' of the mouthpiece from left to right as one ascends from f''', 'the higher the note the stronger the turning' produced an acoustical effect inexplicable to Baermann.[22] This technique may well stem from his father's studies with Franz Tausch and could have been developed to enable the reed-below player to access the highest notes, which had long been the domain of their reed-above counterparts.

Articulation

In the vocabulary of today's clarinettists, the terms 'articulation' and 'tonguing' tend to be virtually synonymous, with players developing high levels of dexterity in single, double and triple tonguing. In contrast, documentary source materials from previous eras suggest that tongued articulation was certainly not the only method used by clarinettists. Roeser's *Essai* is the oldest extant treatise to mention chest articulation, then a necessary by-product of the reed-above embouchure. That the throat was also used in the separation of notes was noted by later reed-above advocates, including Vanderhagen and Lefèvre, as well as Backofen. Since one of the earliest reports of tongued articulation occurred in the same Vanderhagen tutor, we can be fairly certain that contemporary players mixed articulations according to the demands of the music. Just as articulatory nuances have become more uniform throughout the clarinet's lifetime, the way in which these are notated has undergone a similar development.

Reed-above non-tongued articulation

Roeser warned against writing lengthy passages for the clarinet which require rapid articulation, since the chest had to substitute for the tongue stroke. However, Roeser's *Essai* uses no less than five different articulatory signs in its musical examples for clarinet – slurred notes, notes without markings, notes with dots, notes with a wedge and notes with dots under a slur. We must not allow our current preoccupation with obtaining great agility of articulation to make us believe that the chest was somehow inferior, for it must have been capable of producing a range of subtle articulatory nuances. It is more useful simply to read Roeser's account as reporting a technique which was, in some respects, still in its infancy. Indeed Joseph Fröhlich's comments some fifty years later indicated that contemporary reed-above players employed chest articulation with a considerable degree of skill. Vanderhagen, whilst discussing articulation in terms of the tongue stroke, made an exception for the performance of triplets slurred in threes. He specified that the throat, instead of the tongue, be used to mark off the first note, since the use of the tongue in that context would give it too much emphasis. By the early nineteenth century the term 'tongue stroke' had become synonymous with articulation in most French-language sources. It may be that, given the didactic nature of Lefèvre's publication, his counsel against using the throat or chest in separating notes was a warning to less experienced clarinettists.

Fröhlich was the most passionate advocate of the combination of chest articulation and reed-above playing, claiming that it enabled the clarinettist to imitate the singer, 'the only real goal of all instrumentalists'.[23] The tongue was likened to the bow of a string instrument by a large number of commentators on articulation. According to Fröhlich (whose comments are valuable since they document a tradition that has all but vanished), chest articulation also enabled the player to execute rapid passage work and leaps of large intervals between high and low notes. When slurring a group of notes, the first note was to begin with the syllable *ha*, with the lips not held too close together, allowing the free passage of air into the instrument. Fröhlich acknowledged two types of detached sounds; the short and hard, and the soft, more delicate staccato. The first he notated with wedges, instructing the player to hold the lips together whilst still pronouncing the syllable *ha*. The softer staccato was more gently produced by a light striking of the notes with the lips closed as for the slur. This articulation was notated with dots but could also be indicated 'with a small line'.[24] Fröhlich's exercises for the practice of articulation include several from Lefèvre's *Méthode*. Whilst Fröhlich's counsel against the use of the tongue in reed-above playing does seem a little old-fashioned in the light of the highly developed tongued articulation of the contemporary French school, his inclusion of its didactic material provides further proof of his confidence in the use of the chest as an articulatory device.

Reed-above tongued articulation

Tongued articulation may well have been used in conjunction with other types prior to the publication of Vanderhagen's *Méthode* in 1785. Vanderhagen was certainly one of the first sources to notate four different varieties. Firstly, when the notes are left without any indication (nowadays called tongued articulation), Vanderhagen recommended that the player pronounce the voiced consonant ('d') at the beginning of the note. For those marked with *détaché* notated as short dots, he advocated the unvoiced ('t') consonant. When slurring notes in pairs Vanderhagen advised the player to give the first of each pair a little more emphasis. Vanderhagen notated a fourth marking, the *piqué*, with a wedge. This is the shortest of the tongue strokes. Where the slurred notes are the last two in the triplet, a diminuendo was used in order to give emphasis to the first slurred note. In fact, the first note was given the most emphasis in a group of triplets, or any notes beamed together. If the articulation had not been indicated by the composer, Vanderhagen recommended slurring the first two notes and then articulating the rest as tongued notes with the voiced consonant.

Lefèvre's remarks were similar to those of Vanderhagen, but his advice displayed a more practical bias. For example, when playing slurred notes (the *coulé*) the first of which is started with the tongue, Lefèvre instructed the player to keep the lips relaxed in order not to stifle the sound. It was important that the fingers and tongue move together in the *détaché*, which must be carried out with the greatest equality. In this articulation, notated by Lefèvre with a wedge, he recommended pinching the lips and making a strong and forceful tongue stroke. The *piqué* – indicated with a dot – was lighter and executed with less force than the *détaché* or *coupé*. Compared with Vanderhagen's instructions, this stroke was lighter, perhaps indicative of a move towards more refined and subtle articulatory nuances. Lefèvre recommended pronouncing the unvoiced consonant, regardless of the articulation desired. Reed-above tonguing was consolidated in the Neapolitan school of the mid nineteenth century. Sebastiani's *Metodo* confirms most of the instructions given by Lefèvre some fifty years earlier. However, Sebastiani provided an articulation mark that is rare amongst wind methods. The *picchettato*, notated with wedges under a slur for different pitched notes, could also be produced on a sustained note. This effect was indicated by a long note with dots above or below, the number of dots indicating the number of tongue strokes to administer. Gaetano Labanchi, a student of Ernesto Cavallini (probably the most famous reed-above virtuoso), indicated that reed-above tonguing employed at least two methods in the separation of notes. Labanchi's directions for the performance of *legatura* (slurred notes), mentioned that the tongue was not used. *Staccato legato* (indicated by dots under a slur), was produced by tonguing the end of the mouthpiece and articulating a voiced consonant. Ordinary *staccato* (notated with dots), was also produced by tonguing the mouthpiece, but with the unvoiced consonant. The only stroke for which the tongue touched the reed was the *picchettato*, for which each note was well detached from the next. Regardless of reed-position, eighteenth- and nineteenth-century concepts of articulation were concerned not only with the length of a note, but also its weight or volume and its attack. A reflection of today's trend towards homogeneity and conformity has been our preoccupation with the former aspect.

Reed-below tongued articulation

Tongued articulation was used by both reed-above and reed-below clarinettists during the eighteenth and nineteenth centuries, but it was probably first employed exclusively by performers using the latter embouchure. Backofen regarded tongued articulation the most satisfactory of the three methods (tongue, lips and throat) known to him. He recommended beginning accented notes with a strong tongue stroke. Whilst notes marked with a dot were the shortest of detached sounds, those marked with a wedge needed a sharp breath attack. The combination of notes joined by a slur but also marked with a dot meant a light tongue stroke without interrupting the sound. When this combination had a wedge instead of a dot, the tongue stroke was stronger but the sound remained uninterrupted. Although Fröhlich also expressed a preference for the use of tongued articulation in combination with the reed-below embouchure, his comments above seem to indicate that this was not his preferred method.

Because of the commercial thrust of Iwan Müller's *Méthode*, he did not offer extensive comments on articulation. His advice in this area included the direction to 'pay attention to the violin in order to be able to imitate the manner in which it is able to render staccato, legato, sostenuto and the articulations' and to use the syllable *ti* for the tongued notes and *di* for the simple *piqué*.[25] Possibly the earliest instructions regarding double tonguing or *le double coup de langue* are to be found in the *Méthode* of Schneider and Detouches, *c.* 1840. Used in fast movements, this technique was accomplished by pronouncing the syllables *ta-ga-da-ga-da-ga-da* but was not to be misused.[26] Following Backofen, Klosé's instructions represent a consolidation of reed-below tongued articulation. He reiterated the priority that earlier writers gave to the first in a pair of slurred notes. Klosé described two types of detached note: the *pointé simple* or *piqué*, indicated with a dot, and the staccato, indicated with a wedge. The former were executed by a soft tongue stroke, but if the context contained a slur or tie, this also became softer in character. Staccato notes were to be performed in a manner to similar to that indicated by Backofen, with the addition that each note was separated slightly from the next. Baermann notated hard detached notes with a dot, produced with an unvoiced consonant and a sharp short tongue stroke. Softer detached notes, indicated by dots within a slur, were produced delicately, using the voiced consonant. Despite Baermann's claims that detached notes were performed in the same manner whether written with dots or wedges, evidence exists to suggest that those with wedges were executed counter to the hierarchy of the bar.[27]

Fingering

Today's players of the early clarinet are in an unprecedented historical situation. We have at our disposal examples of most of the instruments
in use since the early eighteenth century. It is not unusual for a clarinettist to
perform, say, the Mozart and Weber Quintets on period instruments in the
same concert, despite the radical differences in fingering which must be
accommodated.

Klosé acknowledged that the successful execution of a passage of music
depended upon how it was fingered; his preference for a fluidity of movement was confirmed by later writers including Carl Baermann. Klosé's
introductory remarks concerning the merit of the *clarinette à anneaux
mobiles,* effectively almost identical to the Boehm system in use today, may
convince some of his success in 'reuniting with an equality as perfect as possible in all its compass, a very superior purity of tone and the facility of a
more correct fingering, enabling the performer to play in all the keys indiscriminately'. However, behind this immodest façade lay assumptions that
his clarinet was indeed omnitonic and that homogeneity throughout the
instrument's range was a desirable quality. In contrast, Backofen had
regarded the clarinet's lack of timbral uniformity as an opportunity for
composers and players to exploit its potential for a variety of sonorities.

An excellent starting point for players wishing to become acquainted with
early fingering patterns is an article by Albert Rice which appeared in *The
Galpin Society Journal* in 1984.[28] Rice's examination of fingering charts for
two- to seven-keyed clarinets exposes a remarkable lack of uniformity
during the period of his analysis. Lefèvre's chart for the five-keyed clarinet
gives chromatic fingerings from e to f‴, extending the range diatonically to
c⁗, with alternative fingerings for d‴ and f‴. Backofen's tutor (also for the
five-keyed clarinet), makes a distinction between enharmonic notes. As well
as differentiating notes such as a♯ and b♭, he distinguishes between
fingerings for b♮ and c♭′. Despite this apparent abundance of charts for the
five-keyed clarinet, modern players would do well to take heed of Fröhlich's
advice that it is largely up to individual players to formulate their own
fingerings.

None the less, all three tutors provide assistance for the player in correct-
ing those notes that are unavoidably out of tune. Lefèvre prescribes two remedies for such 'imperfections': the compression of the lips and modifications

to the fingering, also known as 'shading'. His specific examples are drawn from the chalumeau register since the notes of the higher registers 'are usually more accurate and more easily modified'.[29] Fröhlich provided a similar but more extensive critique, covering the range from e to a‴. He added to Lefèvre's remedies with the observation that some notes can be corrected with a softer attack and others by a change in the amount of air pressure. According to Backofen, much could be done to improve the intonation of certain notes by the addition or subtraction of wax to the tone holes. Players needed a good ear in order to be able to make the proper adjustments to their instrument; those who were without this facility should seek the assistance of an experienced string or wind player.

Players who have approached the early clarinet from experience of the Boehm system will find comfort in the following remarks by Backofen. With regard to passages involving a smooth transition from b′ to c♯″, which Roeser warned against using in quick succession, Backofen recommended placing the left hand little finger almost simultaneously on both keys and using a sideways sliding motion to move between them. If the keys were not equidistant from the body of the instrument or were too far apart, then they could easily be bent to render such passages easier to execute! Lefèvre tabulated a number of passages which he felt that composers for the clarinet should avoid altogether (fig. 4. 2). However, he was highly pragmatic and made a typically creative suggestion to assist the smooth execution between c″ and e♭″, prescribing for such contexts a forked fingering for the e♭″ by raising the fourth finger of the right hand and slackening the lip pressure to assist the tuning. Vanderhagen presented two suggestions for executing the over-the-break trill between a′ and b′, the first of which was repeated by Backofen almost twenty years later.[30] Joseph Fröhlich suggested that players consider the advantages of a sixth key for c♯′/g♯″, and mentioned that some instruments had a trill key for b♭′. Backofen recommended as many as four additional keys, citing recent improvements to the flute as justification for such amendments.[31]

Arguably the most significant organological development in nineteenth-century clarinet design was Iwan Müller's thirteen-keyed clarinet.[32] Its rejection by a committee of members of the Paris Conservatoire in 1812 was as much on political as musical grounds. However, as noted in Chapter 2, Müller's instrument soon became popular throughout Europe. His tutor

Fig. 4.2 Table of figures to be avoided by composers for the clarinet, from
J. X. Lefèvre's *Méthode de clarinette* (Paris, 1802)

claimed that, whilst the new system of fingering was 'without contradiction,
the best', those fingerings in established usage had been preserved 'except
where changes were inevitable and very advantageous'.[33] Indeed, a large
proportion of Müller's tutor is a detailed explanation of how to utilise the
keywork of his thirteen-keyed clarinet.

Whereas Müller's design formed the basis for later developments, including those by Baermann, Albert and Oehler, the collaboration between Klosé and Buffet *jeune* had more in common with Theobald Boehm's flute. Clarinettists more familiar with the Boehm-system instrument have often remarked that early clarinet fingerings more closely resemble those of the recorder. For this reason, it is essential that modern players of the period clarinet concentrate on those fingerings most different from those on the Boehm instrument. Klosé remarks concerning 'the execution of leading notes' and employing a 'change of fingering on the same note' afford an insight into the status of issues long since relegated to the periphery of performance practice. When resolving to the tonic, leading notes should ideally be as sharp as possible, similarly if they occur in a melody as part of a concerto or solo.[34] To assist the player in rendering them thus, Klosé provided a 'Table of altered or leading notes and the degrees on which they are found'. However, in ensemble or orchestral performance Klosé suggested that the normal fingerings be used in order better to blend with the other instruments. With the rise of virtuoso violinists during the nineteenth century, wind instrumentalists were keen to appropriate string techniques in order to validate their own aesthetic position. One such technique, which can be rendered on the clarinet 'with a little aptitude', required the use of two different fingerings when a note of the same pitch appeared consecutively. Obviously an attempt to compensate for the apparent uniformity throughout the compass of the *clarinette à anneaux mobiles*, the change of fingering should be as smooth as possible. In the examples given by Klosé, this effect appeared most appropriate with repeated notes separated by a bar-line, particularly in the context of an anacrusis.

Ornamentation

There was considerable divergence amongst clarinet tutors regarding ornamentation, a true reflection of the plethora of musical styles and genres encompassed by the eighteenth and nineteenth centuries. Most tutors dealt with grace notes, trills, mordents and turns. Vanderhagen distinguished two types of long grace note, both notated with a short quaver. The *port de voix* (an ascending appoggiatura) was usually added between two stepwise diatonic notes, and received more dynamic weight than the note it decorated. The note following the *accent* usually descended in pitch, often encompassing a wider interval than the *port de voix*, and was often used on the last note of a bar. Whilst not significantly shorter than the previous two ornaments, a *note de goût* could be slurred to a melody note or used to fill in ascending and descending thirds. However, Vanderhagen warned against its use by individual players within the context of an orchestral tutti to avoid creating 'a bad impression'.[35] He mentioned two different trills or *cadences*. The prepared trill involved leaning a little on the so-called 'loan' note, usually that which is the next highest in pitch, and then accelerating throughout the duration of the note. The unprepared or sudden trill was performed without giving emphasis to the dissonant note. Both trills were indicated by the abbreviation *tr*. The final ornamental device mentioned by Vanderhagen was the mordent or *martellement*, described as opposite to a trill since it borrowed the note below and began on the harmony note. It was written with a small undulating line, now used to denote an inverted mordent.

Although Lefèvre's *Méthode* employed different modes of notation and included additional ornaments, it was more specific concerning particular note lengths. *Petites notes* (or appoggiaturas), were either *au dessous* (from below) or *au dessus* (from above) appoggiaturas. In most cases these received half the value of the following note except for the *petite note préparée*, which was usually preceded by a long note and received half that note's value. Lefèvre also included another type of grace note, the *double petite note*, of which the two notes were either of equal or unequal rhythm. In the latter case the notes were rendered equally and lightly before coming to rest on the next non-ornamental note. It is most likely that during the intervening decades, the term *port de voix* had become the signifier of both ascending and descending grace notes. The context in which Lefèvre presented the *petite note* as indicative of *portamento* or *port de voix* embodied the direction of Vanderhagen's own *port de voix* but both the direction and range of the latter's *accent*. Despite inconsistencies of name and notation, we can be confident that players of taste and intelligence almost certainly refrained from using a *petite note* to decorate the first note of a bar or those preceded by rests.

Lefèvre confirmed Vanderhagen's definition of the trill, which he indicated with either *tr* or an undulating line intercepted half-way along its length with a small vertical line (identical to what is known today as a mordent sign). Lefèvre also recommended beginning the trill on the upper note and giving it an emphasis similar to that prescribed by Vanderhagen. Trills occurring in Andante, Adagio or Largo movements were to be more gently rendered than those in pieces marked Allegro or Presto. A trill occurring at a final cadence, when it was often called the *point d'orgue*, was performed with a termination (often written out). Lefèvre's notation of the trill suggests its acceleration with a crescendo towards the resolution, and he advised that the trilled note itself be given the most force. However, when marked only with an undulating line (like Vanderhagen's *martellement*) a trill became a *mordant* and was really just a truncated trill. Lefèvre's concluding remarks referred the clarinettist to those methods concerned with singing. Likewise for instructions regarding the correct execution of ornaments, Fröhlich referred readers to the Singing Method contained within his comprehensive *Vollständige theoretisch-praktische Musikschule*.

According to Klosé, the grace note was known as the *appoggiatura*. Notated as a small quaver with a line through its tail (that is, a modern *acciaccatura*), the length of each grace note was determined by the note which follows it. In the case of this following note being detached, the appoggiatura received half its value, but two-thirds of the length if succeeded by a non-detached note. Klosé noted that since the appoggiatura note 'is foreign' it needed to be leaned on, as its name implies, and then the sound should diminish 'so that it makes its resolution with softness'.[36] To execute the turn or *gruppetto*, preferably made with the lower semitone as this had a 'softer and more agreeable' effect, one took the value from the preceding note.[37] Klosé cautions against hurrying the turn, or any other ornament. The trill must be 'brilliant, supple, brisk and light', commencing with the main note. A smaller note was added if the trill was to begin on the upper note. When playing a chain of descending trills, the player was advised to use a termination only on the last trill. Whilst Klosé's description of the *mordant* was almost identical to that given by Lefèvre, he added that the most important note was that which carried it, which was to be given more weight than any others.

Klosé regarded Italian music as 'less profound and serious' than that written by Germans and lacking the drama of French music, but expressed considerable certainty that its appeal was to be found in the 'free and facile nature' of Italian song, and principally in the manner with which it was ornamented with 'so much grace and taste'.[38] Whilst such remarks betray some national chauvinism, they are certainly amongst Klosé's most informative in relation to ornamentation. To assist the French player in appropriating some of these desirable mannerisms, he presented nine different embellishments of an eight-bar melody.

Carl Baermann described both the long and the short appoggiatura or *Vorschlag*. The longer of the two, indicated by a longer note, was strongly accented. If it occurred before a note longer than a quaver it took half that note's value, but could be even longer if written before a tied note. When performing the short *Vorschlag*, the player should accent the main note. Since the shorter ornament, with its correspondingly short note value (like both Klosé's *appoggiatura* and the modern *acciaccatura*), did not occur 'in the music of the old masters', Baermann advised the clarinettist to defer to their 'taste, experience and correct understanding of the passages to be interpreted' in order to render a note of the appropriate length.[39] Although acknowledging trills that began on the upper note as well as the trill note itself, Baermann expressed a preference for the latter. The trill was notated with the usual marking, those without a termination indicated by both the *tr* and undulating line. He advised that all trills should end with a termination, but those occurring in pieces of music with slow tempi or sostenuto passages should accelerate and have a slower termination. Baermann reminds us that the best judge in such cases must be the player's own refined and artistic taste.

Confusingly for modern players, Baermann used the term *Pralltriller* to describe the mordent, and *Mordent* to specify a turn. He advised that in the music of composers of previous eras, the *Pralltriller* was performed in the manner of Vanderhagen's *martellement*, but in Baermann's time it was executed as instructed by Lefèvre and Klosé. The *Mordent* was used to excess by earlier composers 'but this situation has been entirely remedied by our modern school of composers', proclaimed Baermann. When indicated on a dotted note, the last note of the turn received the value of the dot. Baermann included a realisation of the turns in bar 71 of the Larghetto from Mozart's Clarinet Quintet, in which the progression c″, d″, c″, b′ is notated in demisemiquavers and the final c″ and d″ are semiquavers. As a general rule he suggested that turns on the tonic or dominant ought to be to the semitone below, but despaired that 'too many signs cause confusion'.[40]

Other practical and aesthetic considerations

In 1764 Valentin Roeser (*Essai d'instruction*, p. 2) listed clarinets in G, A, B♭, C, D, E and F. Whilst the clarinets in A, B♭, C and D were the most common, the higher pitched ones in E and F were used in orchestral pieces of a more consistently loud dynamic. The low G clarinet was a rarity, distinguishable by its sweet timbre. Fröhlich claimed that a clarinettist should be able to play in all keys on one instrument but acknowledged the need for a variety of clarinets to accommodate the many impure notes on each instrument. Of those clarinets used in orchestral playing, Fröhlich mentioned the A as having a soft character and a timbre not unlike that of the basset horn and bassoon. By 1843, Klosé was declaring that he had rid the clarinet world of the 'onerous and troublesome' need for players to have three instruments (pitched in C, B♭ and A)! Despite the obvious refinements manifest in the *clarinette à anneaux mobiles*, Klosé's claim that its potential included 'the faculty of playing in all the keys on one instrument' can be regarded as somewhat exaggerated. His suggestion that composers for the clarinet ought exclusively to write for the B♭ clarinet in the C clef apparently did not find favour with his contemporaries.

The didactic material presented within the tutors varies according to the writer's specific purpose. Lefèvre's work is the most comprehensive of the earlier tutors, with exercises for finger agility and articulation in key signatures of up to two sharps and four flats. He also includes twelve progressive clarinet sonatas, which according to his instructions could be performed on the B♭ clarinet with downward transposition of the bass line.[41] This serves to confirm Backofen's comment that the French preferred the C clarinet upon which to learn the instrument. Backofen's tutor recommended that the teacher use a violin in playing duets with the pupil, only changing to the clarinet when the pupil has perfected the part. Following several solo exercises to familiarise the student with particular keys and patterns of articulation, Backofen includes some duets for clarinet and cello, and for two clarinets.

Vanderhagen's *Méthode* does not include extensive pieces for technical study, but presents a few short pieces with programmatic titles, as well as several duets. The didactic material included by Klosé includes exercises in all keys, a wide variety of scales and arpeggios, together with studies for the refining of various articulations and different registers of the instrument. This latter material is presented as solos and duets. Whilst Klosé encouraged the use of his *Méthode* by players of the thirteen-keyed clarinet, the reasons for his inclusion of over one hundred exercises on passages 'which are only executed with difficulty on the thirteen-keyed clarinet, but which become simple and easy on the Boehm clarinet' are not difficult to imagine.[42] Equally telling is his advice that four hours' practice 'ought to be sufficient' for the clarinettist! [43] The nature of the exercises presented by Baermann is similar to those in Klosé with the exception of those specifically designed to fine-tune the finger technique of the player of the Baermann-system clarinet.

Lefèvre regarded breathing and phrasing as particularly important to the tasteful rendering of music. It is essential that both aspects be subordinated to the musical rhythm, in order to preserve the meaning of a particular phrase. If it is not possible to play an entire phrase in one breath, a suitable place to breathe must be intelligently sought. For further clarification, he provides notated examples of such places. Baermann adopts a similarly rigorous and prescriptive approach to breathing, even indicating places to breathe with his own symbol (not unlike that of a minim with a quaver tail). While much of his advice follows Lefèvre, Baermann also counsels against breathing before a leading note or other note of resolution. His recommendation that, for the sake of greater expressive freedom, more frequent breaths can be indulged in particularly in passages requiring a more impulsive or intensive feeling has a particular resonance for the performer of clarinet music of the Romantic repertory. A similar technique was mentioned by Klosé under the heading of 'demi-respiration', which he described as 'a pleasing effect in taking slower certain notes to which one wishes to give a particular shade or expression', recommending its use for detached notes or after the first note of a bar.[44]

Lefèvre's *Méthode* makes pertinent remarks on how to perform Adagio and Allegro movements. The Adagio is possibly the most difficult type of piece to play, since without the necessary sensitivity to the sentiments of the music, no performer can hope to succeed in reaching an adequate expression. This is achieved by varying the nuance and articulation of the notes, and by the use of correct and appropriate breathing to give each phrase its own distinctive quality. Apart from possessing an inherent talent and being diligent in the area of personal practice, the artist must also spend time listening to the most skilled musicians and adopt their methods where appropriate, advice reiterated sixty years later by Baermann.[45] The Allegro makes similar demands of the player, and must be performed energetically and gracefully. The instrumentalist is responsible for varying the dynamics on the repeat of a phrase. If the same phrase is to be repeated further, one ought to change the articulations as well. Such amendments serve to ensure that the piece is rendered with brilliance and monotony is avoided.

According to Klosé, a good clarinettist performs a phrase according to the following principles: the first bars will be well poised and well accented in accordance with the musical meaning and the end of the phrase rendered with spirit and panache. The first note should be emphasised in nuance and length since this gives to those that follow a warmer and more animated character; although often indicated by an accent mark, such first notes are not to be interpreted in that manner. In acknowledging the notational short-comings of expression marks, Baermann implied that a certain degree of freedom is allowed the player, provided one is appropriately tasteful. Amongst his general principles of musical interpretation, Baermann made the following points: one should play everything exactly as written, observing all markings, having first decided upon the various reasons for their use oneself; incorrect phrasing is to be avoided as it corrupts musical meaning; unaccented notes, unless marked staccato, are played broadly; the player should be aware of accented notes, of which the most important is the first of every bar; and one must not hurry the last notes in a bar, particularly those connected with the musical idea of the following bar. Baermann's remark that the steady beat of the metronome is intolerable in certain passages reflects a sentiment also expressed by Brahms.[46] Tempo flexibility was for the more advanced player, guided by refined taste and intuition, and chamber musicians should adapt their playing to the whole ensemble. By implication, Baermann advocated the old practice of lifting at the end of a slur, since in the context of two notes slurred together, only the first was to receive its full value. Ideally, ascending notes should be rendered with increased emotion and *vice versa*. In order not to be guilty of playing the music of Mozart in the manner of Beethoven, betraying 'a lamentable lack of musical understanding', it was necessary to study the works of 'the great masters according to their individuality'.[47] In the light of these remarks, it seems highly likely that if Baermann were alive today, he would almost certainly ascribe the homogeneity of many of today's players to their lack of musical versatility and the narrow knowledge base from which many unquestioningly operate!

'Without the necessary gradations of light and shade music would be pale and uncoloured; for melody requires expression as the earth requires light, as the body needs a soul', wrote Klosé. For him, taste revealed the true artist, and musicians who possessed it were able to interpret music meaningfully and impart its message to their audience. In these circumstances music 'attains a role far more imposing; it becomes a language strong, energetic and potent, which impresses the heart, silences the multitude, and leads them to great and noble actions'.[48]

5   The language of musical style

Introduction

Among all wind instruments, none approaches the tone of the full, female soprano voice as much as does the clarinet. Its richness of tone, which on the one hand approaches the powerful clarino, and on the other, the pleasant, gentle quality that can be played at a level hardly audible, as an echo, gives the clarinet the ability of projecting every kind of expression which the composer might wish to assign to it. In force and richness it reigns as a solo instrument in playing brilliant passages, to which its innate mellowness offers a beautiful contrast, while it is also able to adjust to any kind of character as an accompanying instrument. In the orchestra, it maintains a penetrating fullness and, at the same time, couples softness with it.[1]

Fröhlich's enthusiasm for the clarinet dates from the era of Weber's concertos and is representative of the praise the instrument has inspired throughout its history. Yet an important caveat had already been issued by Lefèvre, who warned that clarinet playing could quickly become monotonous without appropriate nuance of sound and articulation. He stated that it was not sufficient merely to read the notes and play the music, for the clarinettist must identify its character and not be constrained by the notation. Lefèvre commented that a certain coldness and monotony had often been attributed to the instrument, which was in fact the responsibility of the player.[2] As noted in the previous chapter, Lefèvre offered specific advice on the musical requirements of Adagio and Allegro movements, but in later nineteenth-century publications, technical considerations were gradually to overwhelm this kind of artistic approach inherited from the previous century.

Sources
As we have already implied, today's period performer must be prepared to absorb a variety of primary source material, much of it not directly

related to the clarinet. Historical instruments offer an opportunity to enter more closely into the sound-world of a particular composer. We have already considered those aspects of a composer's music which he did not find it necessary to write down; an earlier musician's way of communicating will always for us remain a foreign language. But when we become able to express ourselves freely within it, we can certainly achieve an enhanced range of expression. As an illustration, the original nuances of a classical, articulated style are worth re-capturing not merely for historical reasons but also for their aesthetic benefit; in classical documents, expressive performance is consistently seen as the result of attention to detail.

In order to achieve the whole range of expression intended by a composer, all the stylistically relevant information must be investigated; this can help to fill the vast gap between what is contained in the score and its execution. Familiarity with the musical language of an earlier time can provide a framework for interpretation and guidelines to the many choices available within a style, as well as to the types of freedom and ambiguities. At its best, performance can be the completion of the creative process, exhibiting both conviction and spontaneity.

The science of music is well documented by the theorists; music as an art is more difficult to explain. We need at least to be aware of philosophical treatises on other instruments by Quantz (flute, 1752), Leopold Mozart (violin, 1756), C. P. E. Bach (keyboard, 1753 and 1762), Türk (keyboard, 1789) and Tromlitz (flute, 1791), amongst others. Naturally, no single source can ever be regarded as definitive in any particular area. These authors were individual musicians working in different parts of Europe, who often disagreed with one another in a quite stimulating way. Some musical matters, such as the interpretation of certain rhythms or how to play trills, were as controversial then as now; indeed, answers to many musical questions were not as standardised as we might sometimes want to pretend nowadays.

Rhetoric

Clarinettists in general tend to have rather a tarnished reputation in relation to style, arguably because of the predominance of legato in modern playing. In analysing the technique of flute playing, Quantz assigns great importance to the tongue, by which animation is given to the execution of notes, by analogy with the various violin bow-strokes. The sheer range of articulation implied by his description of music as an artificial language is vast. In emphasising the twin ideals of knowledge and taste, Quantz warned against a teacher who understands nothing of harmony, and who is no more than an instrumentalist. Industry founded upon an ardent love and insatiable enthusiasm for music must be fuelled by constant and diligent inquiry.

In assuming a good knowledge of harmony and the art of singing, eighteenth-century writers were in fact expecting that the performer would glean a great deal of interpretative information from the rhythm, melodic intervals, phrasing and harmony notated in the score, and adapt his technique accordingly. Leopold Mozart lays special emphasis on the importance of adherence to the written and prescribed slurs. He states that within a slur, 'the first of such united notes must be somewhat strongly stressed, but the remainder slurred on to it quite smoothly and more and more quietly'.[3] As for notes without slurs, C. P. E. Bach offers the significant (if somewhat extreme) comment that they should be played half length as a matter of course. This was qualified by the general remark that the briskness of allegros was expressed in detached notes and the tenderness of adagios by broad, slurred notes – in other words, the articulation must always serve the characterisation. In terms of harmony, the general rule was that dissonances must be played loudly and consonances softly, since the former arouse our emotions and the latter quieten them. Melodic inflection also derives from the hierarchy of notes within the bar and the context of chromatic notes. Character and taste are also high on Leopold Mozart's list of priorities; a tasteful performance can only be learned from sound judgement and long experience. All treatises pay great attention to ornamentation in general and the appoggiatura in particular, and their role in achieving appropriate characterisation. Conversely, Quantz has a list of examples of poor execution which includes untrue intonation, forced tone, notes executed indistinctly, notes slurred indiscriminately, non-observance of tempo, inaccurate note-values, poor preparation and resolution of dissonances, and performance without feeling or sentiment. In addition to these general remarks relating to characterisation and articulation, all the treatises contain a mine of varied and detailed musical advice; Mozart, for example, comments that a note with a pause must be allowed to diminish and die,[4] whilst Quantz states that a wind cadenza should be playable in a single breath.[5]

For the beginner, Quantz recommends a practice schedule of two hours each morning and afternoon; with but an hour a day, profit may be slow in coming. His idealism, together with the value of his many universal truths, is best seen in his chapter on 'What must be observed in public concerts'. The player must find out whether his audience are connoisseurs or amateurs; in order to ingratiate oneself with them, one must know their humours. This is an area where recording and large concert halls have placed 'authenticity' beyond reach. Quantz usefully notes that the size of room and the acoustic will affect both dynamic and execution.

According to Quantz, tempo can be deduced from the human pulse (a method used from the late sixteenth century until the invention of the metronome during Beethoven's lifetime). Five basic tempo groups were commonly identified and described in ways which reinforce the association of sentiment and performance style with tempi: Largo (slow), Adagio (moderately slow), Andante (walking, the middle way between fast and slow), Allegro (quick) and Presto (very fast). Of these, Adagio and Andante have probably undergone the greatest change, becoming a great deal slower during the nineteenth century. The interaction of time-signature, note values and tempo heading determined choice of tempo. Large note values implied heavier execution, whilst each time-signature had its own characterisation; as the value of the fraction decreased (e.g. 3/2 to 3/4, 3/8 or 3/16), the liveliness of tempo or execution would increase. This has implications for the 3/8 Andante of Mozart's C minor Wind Serenade K388, for example. Harmonic rhythm, construction of the texture, degree and types of articulation were all important indicators.

Significantly, Quantz warns composers to avoid extremes of tonality in writing for wind instruments (relevant to the eighteenth-century clarinet to an even greater extent than the flute). Taking for granted an unequally tempered scale, Quantz advises that notes indicated with flats are to be played a little sharper than those with sharps, e.g. E♭ versus D♯. This has important implications for the baroque repertory, and Tromlitz later confirms that among flautists the tempered scale was retained throughout much of the eighteenth century. Quantz insists that a player must have a good understanding of the proportion of intervals in the scale, and despite the obvious necessity for a fine instrument, the player is ultimately more important. This remains excellent advice. Lefèvre remarks that because the same clarinet fingering is used for enharmonic notes, the player must use his ear for the correct pitching of notes, tightening or loosening the lips according to the tonalities encountered in the music.[6] Carl Baermann admitted that no clarinet could play perfectly in tune, but observed that every musician was aware that the major third of A major was distinguishable from the minor third of B♭ minor.[7]

Of sources later than Quantz, the important *Clavierschule* by Daniel Gottlob Türk dates from 1789, the year Mozart composed his Clarinet Quintet. As already noted, Türk was well acquainted with the works of Mozart and performed them frequently. His chapter on execution both summarises and elaborates upon the work of earlier writers; characterisation and *affekt* are discussed at length, whilst articulation continues to be an important area, 'the emphasis which certain tones receive and . . . the proper connection and separation of musical periods'. In reading poetry, certain words or syllables must be emphasised to make it comprehensible to the listener. His definition of melodic inflection takes careful account of both melodic and harmonic context, with special attention to the role of dissonance. Türk again compares music with speech: 'as the latter may be divided into smaller and larger parts or members, so this is also true of music. A main section of a composition is approximately the same as that which is understood as a complete part in a speech. A musical period or section . . . would be like that which is called a period in speech and which is separated from that which follows by a full-stop.'[8] Smaller units are equivalent to colon, semicolon and comma. Türk discusses at some length the detachment, sustaining and slurring of notes, to be related to the prevailing character of the music. He remarks that the half-length recommended by Bach for unslurred notes is too short, and fails to allow for differences in character, or for the difference between staccato and normal notes. Character determines the treatment of dotted rhythms, where the longer note tends to be prolonged. Tempo is also crucial; slowness makes for feeble and dull performance, while excessive speed causes loss of clarity and spoils the intended effect.

Türk affirms that it is by means of his expression that a true master will distinguish himself noticeably from the average musician. Expression presupposes a broad range of knowledge and above all, a sensitive soul. Some musical subtleties cannot really be described – they must be heard. Works of art lose much if what is natural in them is missed; if music is given a forced or timid performance, the composer's purpose is only half achieved. Furthermore, repertory should be chosen which lies within one's capabilities, though no one will manage to play well at all times and in all circumstances, since the disposition of one's spirits has a very marked influence on performance.

The interpretation of appoggiaturas continued to be a preoccupation of classical theorists, the general consensus being that notation was insufficiently precise (none of the great composers left instructions for their interpretation). Türk notes their use by composers to provide more continuity, charm, vitality and lyricism, and to give the harmony more variety by intermingling dissonances. Long appoggiaturas take half the following note value, or two-thirds of a dotted note; however, for the sake of uniformity and for harmonic reasons they sometimes only take a third in the latter case. This is an important point in relation to the Adagio of Mozart's Clarinet Concerto. Appoggiaturas are always slurred and played with greater emphasis than the main note. On short appoggiaturas C. P. E. Bach and some contemporaries demand emphasis, whereas Leopold Mozart suggests the opposite. Türk lists ten contexts in which the appoggiatura must be short, which provide useful information for decisions in Mozart, as well as other classical composers for the clarinet such as Vanhal.

Türk was much occupied with ornamentation (both notated and improvised), stating that one should be guided by the character of their context. Speed of trill, for example, might be affected by the acoustic. Trills begin on the upper note, and in a chain of trills, each can have a termination. His chapter on improvised ornamentation needs to be read by any historically aware clarinettist, especially in relation to the slow movements of Mozart's Clarinet Quintet and Concerto. Baroque improvisation was still widely practised, and Türk's first thought is that any additions should suit the prevailing character; a sorrowful Adagio, for example, demands something other than a merry embellishment. Transitional pauses (as in the Concerto's first movement) should have a short decoration; cadenzas proper should be played as if invented on the spur of the moment. Elsewhere, extempore embellishments must be used sparingly and in the right place:

> Since the art of variation presumes, in addition to a great deal of knowledge of harmony, a very refined taste, good judgement, skill

in execution, security in counting &c., only an accomplished master, and only when he is well disposed, should attempt to include ornaments of this kind . . . Only those places should be varied (but only when the composition is repeated) which would otherwise not be interesting enough and consequently become tedious . . . particularly in an Adagio.[9]

Any elaboration must appear to have been achieved with ease, and

those passages which in themselves are already of striking beauty or liveliness, as well as compositions in which sadness, seriousness, noble simplicity, solemn and lofty greatness, pride and the like, are predominant characteristics should be completely spared from variations and elaborations, or these should be used very sparingly and with suitable discrimination. There are certain compositions or individual sections which are so communicative and speak so directly to the heart of the listener, without any false glitter, that in such cases a beautiful tone corresponding to the character of the music, played softly or more strongly, are the only means by which the expression should be made more intense.[10]

These comments have a special relevance to Mozart's clarinet music.

The Romantic era

The beginning of the nineteenth century saw many musical changes which reflected the social climate. Public concerts became an important focus for social life, taking place in ever larger halls. Improved communications meant that virtuosi could travel and stimulate musical life, whilst the foundation of institutions such as the Paris Conservatoire encouraged higher technical standards. Teachers helped to establish repertory, and standardisation in important areas such as pitch began slowly to develop. For orchestras – such as the self-governing Leipzig Gewandhaus under Mendelssohn – this was an era of exciting developments. Weber and Spohr were among the first generation of baton conductors. On the other hand, during a period of radical musical developments, standards were extremely variable. At this period legato certainly became a more pervasive feature, though not to the extent to which we have become accustomed. Some useful indicators for this period, which encompasses the careers of Beethoven and Schubert as well as Weber and Spohr, are treatises for the major solo instruments such as violin and piano. Czerny wrote of his piano studies that Beethoven 'made me especially aware of the legato, of which he himself had control to such an incomparable degree and which all other pianists at that time considered impossible on the fortepiano; the chopped and smartly detached playing [of Mozart's time] was still fashionable'.[11] In 1852 Czerny further conveyed Beethoven's own impressions: 'he had heard Mozart play; Mozart had a delicate but choppy touch, with no legato, which Beethoven at first found very strange, since he was accustomed to treat the fortepiano like the organ'.[12] Beethoven's own sonatas begin to reveal large-scale slurs over several bars, in addition to the small-scale articulations contained within a bar. Parallel examples may be found in Weber's clarinet music. None the less, there is no evidence whatsoever that the rhetorical aspect of music was abandoned at a stroke. Indeed, a work such as Baillot's violin treatise of 1834 makes it clear that the essential principles of musical expression were still intact.

Baillot states that it is not enough to be born sensitive; the player must bear with his soul that expansive force, that warmth of feeling which spreads out from itself and imparts itself to others, penetrates, burns. True expression depends on sound quality, movement, style, taste, precision, and genius of execution. Characterisation remains important, as does awareness of style. Taste continues to be a preoccupation, requiring thought as much as instinct. Baillot's remarks on precision are perhaps his most important; it is not sufficient to keep time strictly from bar to bar, since each subdivision must also be observed. Expression sometimes allows for a slight alteration in the time, but either this is graduated and virtually imperceptible, or the beat is simply disguised. If such freedom is abused, the piece can soon lose its charm and character. The difficulty of playing precisely is obvious when one tries to play with the aid of a metronome.

> In order to succeed, the head must be accustomed early to moderate the liveliness of the senses and to regulate those passions which must move the performer; if he allows himself to be carried away by them, there will no longer be any sense of the beat, nuances, nor

pleasing effects; if he is too reserved, his performance will be cold;
art consists in maintaining a balance between the feelings that
carry you away and those which hold you back; as one can see, this
is a different kind of precision from that which aims solely at the
exact division of the beat and bar; it is the result as much of good
practice as of maturity of talent.[13]

Baillot's message is that a player's sensibility holds the key to an inexhaust-
ible source of expression, which must however be disciplined in its execution.

Spohr's violin method of 1832 is a source even closer to the clarinet repertoire. He too discusses style in some detail, including consideration of
different performing situations. A player must impart spiritual life to the
work he is performing, in an interpretation which combines accuracy, sensibility and elegance. He advises steadiness of tempo, yet subject to the
confines of taste allows speeding up of the tempo in fiery and impassioned
passages, together with holding back in those which have a tender or sad,
melancholy character. Significantly, Weber wrote of the metronome marks
to his *Euryanthe*: 'The beat should not be a tyrannical restriction or the
driving of a mill-hammer. On the contrary, it should be to the music what
the pulse beat is to the life of man.'[14]

How far did the principles of classical phrasing survive into the nineteenth century? Baillot continues to use the analogy of speech, where a sen-
tence is constructed to give shape to an idea, and punctuation aids
understanding of the message. Nuance is the basic element in musical
expression, providing phrases with colour and character. Melodic inflection
continued to be governed by harmonic considerations, including prolonga-
tion of first notes within a slur or dissonances within the phrase.
Nineteenth-century composers in general phrased their clarinet music with
some care and attention (Brahms is a fine example), and there is good reason
to suppose that they expected an articulated approach from the small-scale
as well as the large-scale slurs. (In the classical period, longer slurs had not
yet acquired the specific purpose of designating phrase-lengths; this arose as
an expression of the developing cantabile melodic style that naturally led to
more extensive cantabile playing, in Beethoven and others).

Nevertheless, there were some important stylistic developments at the beginning of the nineteenth century. Ornamentation had gradually changed from its baroque function of achieving continuity to a classical function of articulating structure, the retention of trills (e.g. at the end of concerto expositions and recapitulations) being significant. Other ornaments became rarer and thematic, even the trill losing its ornamental status in late Beethoven, becoming an essential motif or suspension of rhythm. Though the late baroque practice of upper-note trills was recorded by C. P. E. Bach, there were dissenters, and the non-cadential trills preserved via mechanical clocks associated with Haydn have main-note trills. Some writers around the turn of the century maintained that the trill should be begun according to the taste of the performer, whilst Adam's piano method (1804) for the Paris Conservatoire preferred main-note starts from Bach to Beethoven, with a few exceptions. Koch's *Lexicon* of 1802 noted disagreement among music teachers, most preferring an upper-note start; significantly he remarked that for the soloist, the issue was of no special significance. Türk's second edition (1802), Clementi and even Starke's Piano School of 1819 remained conservative in their remarks. Beethoven was aware of both types of trill, preferring main-note starts where advantageous melodic flow (and often dissonance) was created. Indeed, the overall trend was in favour of the main note, and Hummel stated in 1828 that this was the general rule. The best guide must be melodic contour and harmonic considerations; however much we may regret it, no definite rules can be applied.

Another ambiguous area is that of dotted rhythms and mixed metres (e.g. two against three). During the later eighteenth century, the performance and notation of these rhythms gradually became more literal and accurate, but this process of change left many uncertainties, examples from clarinet works ranging from the Handel *Ouverture* (discussed as a case study in Chapter 6) to Schubert's *Shepherd on the Rock*. C. P. E. Bach noted that in combination with triplets, dotted rhythms were 'rationalised', and with few exceptions this remained general baroque practice. In early classical music, two against three (or even three against four) became fashionable in the works of certain composers (including Telemann). In Türk's view this remained a beauty to which one must first become accustomed in order to find it tolerable. He advised performance of the short note after the third triplet, and this was also Czerny's view, though Starke in 1819 continued to argue in favour of assimilation. As a practical guide, tempo, character and the roles of the rhythms involved all have a bearing, as does the amount of weight allotted to the small note after the dot. As for the general treatment of dotted rhythms, Türk argues in favour of variety according to context; Hummel remarked upon an exercise consisting entirely of dotted rhythms that it must be played with a good deal of point (*etwas pikant*).

Notwithstanding these examples, there was a tendency for scores to be notated in more detail, as music became disseminated more widely and musicians were able to travel more easily. Tempo markings were a significant example; for Beethoven, tempo was an inherent part of the character of a composition, and he attempted to define new tempos by extensive use of additional clauses to express the mood of a piece. Though it is not known how Beethoven arrived at his metronome indications, their consistent brisk-ness continues to prove controversial today. The trend for fast movements to be played increasingly quickly seems to have continued during and after Beethoven's lifetime, particularly in Central Europe. It was Liszt and Wagner who reversed this position, the latter's conducting becoming a dominant force throughout Europe, imbuing his entire repertoire with emotional, even sentimental significance.

As we have noted throughout this book, early recordings can help to illu-minate the spontaneity of late nineteenth-century performance practice. Another special source for Brahms interpretation is the *Violinschule* (Berlin, 1902–5), co-written by the composer's friend Joseph Joachim. He acknowl-edged that a work by Bach or Tartini demanded a different style of delivery from one by Mendelssohn or Spohr, the intervening century bringing not just a great difference with regard to form but also with regard to delivery; however, this would not at that time have involved a change of violin or bow. It is clear from a correspondence in 1879 between Brahms and Joachim that Brahms followed classical composers in regarding the shortening of the second of a pair of notes as obligatory, whereas in longer phrases it was optional. A famous instance of such paired quavers occurs at bar 47 of the Adagio of the Clarinet Quintet, and there are several examples at the begin-ning of the E♭ Sonata. Although Mühlfeld's playing was never the subject of extended discourse among his admirers, the playing of both Brahms and Joachim was described in detail by their contemporaries. Joachim's biogra-pher J. A. Fuller Maitland observed that his regulated or logical freedom was based on the principle of the agogic accent, i.e.

the kind of accent that consists, not of an actual stress or intensification of tone on the note, but of a kind of lengthening out of its time value, at the beginning of the bar, and at points where a secondary accent may be required. All the greatest interpreters of the best music have been accustomed to play this kind of accent on the first note of the bar, or of a phrase, as taste may suggest, but none have ever carried out the principle so far or with such fine results as Joachim has done.[15]

Such an intimate engagement with the surface detail of the music might well stand as a model for players of other instruments in this area of the repertory, not least the clarinet.

6   Case studies in ensemble music

The following case studies aim primarily to draw attention to some of the issues which might be addressed in performance. Illuminating period clarinet playing demands a certain attitude of mind, so that there can be no special prescription for playing any particular piece of music. Naturally, stylistic considerations can be stimulating for the player of the modern clarinet, as well as for specialists on historical instruments.

Handel : *Ouverture* HWV 424 for two clarinets and horn

Genesis and reception

Handel's extraordinary *Ouverture* for 'Clarinet 1', 'Clarinet 2' and 'Corno da caccia' is the only music Handel is known to have written for the clarinet.[1] The autograph in the Fitzwilliam Museum, Cambridge (Sign. 30. H. 14) has the names of the instruments entered by Handel's friend and amanuensis John Christopher Smith, senior.[2] For some time it was believed that the three parts formed the concertino of a more lavishly-scored work, whose string parts were lost.[3] However, they are indeed self-sufficient and the unusual scoring strongly suggests that the piece was composed for the travelling Hungarian horn-player mysteriously known only as Mr Charles. He was active in London from 1734 and paid a visit to Dublin in 1742, overlapping with Handel's season there. In addition to the horn, his concerts often featured the clarinet and 'shalamo' (chalumeau), which he played in ensembles with his 'second', his pupils and members of his family. An announcement in the *Dublin Mercury* for his first Irish concert on 12 May 1742 boasted; 'N. B. The Clarinet, the Hautbois de Amour, and Shalamo, were never heard in this Kingdom before.' Further details of the career and travels of Mr Charles have recently been documented in some detail.[4]

Handel's clarinet writing illustrates why the instrument was called 'clarinetto' or little 'clarino', the term used for high-register trumpet idioms; but he also shows awareness of the clarinet's potential for cantabile which was to be exploited by succeeding generations of composers. The opening movement is in the style of a French overture and was later re-worked by Handel in his *Concerto a due cori* no. 3 of 1747. The Larghetto establishes a contrasting pastoral mood, generating an attractive cadential phrase which Handel later took up in the closing chorus of Act 2 of *Semele*. A theme from Giovanni Porta's opera *Numitore* (1720) provides the basis for the fanfare motif heading the fourth movement; it also appears in Handel's *Samson* (1741, 1742) and he used it again in the Act III Sinfonia in *Solomon* (1749) known as 'The Arrival of the Queen of Sheba'.

Demonstration that the surviving material for the *Ouverture* was indeed complete took place more than two hundred years later in a flurry of diverse scholarly and practical activity. In 1950 *The Galpin Society Journal* carried an article on Handel and the clarinet,[5] coinciding with the recording (on B♭ clarinets sounding in C major) by the London Baroque Ensemble on a 78 rpm disc (Parlophone R20581), whose members on that occasion consisted of Frederick Thurston, Gervase de Peyer and Dennis Brain. The Ensemble's director Karl Haas published a score and parts in 1952 (Schott 5553). Subsequently the work appeared in the Hallische Händel-Ausgabe (vol. IV/15, Kassel, 1979) and was subsequently recorded on period instruments by L'Ecole d'Orphée (CRD 1082, 1985) and by Keith Puddy and colleagues (Clarinet Classics CC0004, 1993).

Source

The sole primary source is the autograph, whose manuscript bears watermarks confirming the traditional date of *c.* 1740 assigned to the work.[6] The edition by Terence Best for the Hallische Händel-Ausgabe adds only one or two modest editorial slurs and trills, for the sake of consistency. These details are clearly differentiated from Handel's own text. Best's commentary summarises the essential background to the music, whilst drawing attention to the main issues of performance practice inherent in Handel's music. Haas remains a useful practical edition and all his suggestions relating to dynamics are editorial, as his preface points out. Handel's original text contains virtually no small-scale slurs, except in bars 10 (clarinets 1 and 2) and 22 (clarinet 1) in the fugal Allegro; Haas's longer phrase-markings in bars 32–6 are also of his own invention.[7] As for actual pitches and rhythms, we may note the following divergences:

	bar	Haas	Best
[Andante]	21, 2nd note, clt 2	a′	d″
	24, 4th crotchet, clt 2	g♯′	b′
	24, 4th crotchet, hn	e″	d″
Allegro	32, beginning, clt 2[8]	crotchet + quaver rest	dotted crotchet
Larghetto	3, final note, clt 1	g″	f♯″

Performance practice

The demanding horn part is playable without hand-stopping on a small-belled baroque instrument of the type made *c*. 1720 by the Viennese family Leichnamschneider. As already noted, the surviving D clarinet in Nuremberg by Jacob Denner is the type of instrument which seems well suited to Handel's music.[9] However, it was asserted in 1950 that a C clarinet might also be a possibility for the *Ouverture*.[10] Forty years later, Rice found himself in agreement: 'Indeed, on the basis of our working knowledge of clarinet fingerings, it is also apparent that these parts were playable on certain two-key clarinets in *c*′ and three-key clarinets in *d*′.'[11] But in fact, it would have been highly unusual for any clarinet piece of this date not to have been written in its tonic key; it is significant that each movement of the *Ouverture* is in D major. The already steep technical demands of Handel's music become almost insuperable on any surviving C clarinet of the period.

Handel requires a number of chromatic notes which on two-keyed D clarinets vary both in quality and in colour. These include f♯′, g♯′, b♭′, c♯′, f♯″ (all sounding a tone higher); c♯″ poses special problems, requiring accurate half-holing of R4 in a number of different contexts. Another challenge is to produce consistently the note b, which achieves some prominence in the Larghetto and involves half-holing R1. This finger technique appears regularly in flute tutors of the period, for example Hotteterre (*c*. 1728) and Quantz (1752). Another difficulty below the break is that, rather confusingly for the modern player, Denner's front key produces b♭′, the speaker a′ and both together b′. The fingering charts for two-keyed clarinets by Majer (1732) and Eisel (1738) are thoroughly investigated and compared by Rice (pp. 64–71). Their information needs to be supplemented by a considerable degree of individual experiment.

Ex. 6.1 Handel, *Ouverture* for two clarinets and horn, [Andante], bars 17–19

The sheer variety of colours inherent in a period performance can scarcely be recreated even in a stylish rendition with Boehm clarinets and valve horn. On the other hand, the element of wild abandon implied within Handel's faster movements raises the question of the circumstances of the première and indeed whether outdoor performance may even have been intended. This is a piece which calls into question the relationship between historical performance and the extremes of clarity and accuracy routinely demanded by the culture of the compact disc. As we have noted in earlier chapters, the baroque clarinet was played with reed against the top lip and articulation achieved variously by means of the chest, throat or tongue. There is considerable scope here for individual research, and the treatise of 1764 by Valentin Roeser is an especially important source, since he began his career in Germany.

The musical notation of Handel's *Ouverture* is not quite as straightforward as might at first appear to be the case. Dotted rhythms of French overtures were routinely exaggerated, most of the evidence for this overdotting emanating from mid-eighteenth-century German theorists. Agricola declares that 'Short notes after a dot . . . are always played very short and at the very end of their value', while C. P. E. Bach states: 'Short notes which follow dotted ones are always shorter in execution than their notated length.' Leopold Mozart writes: 'Dotted notes must be held somewhat longer, but the time taken up by the extended value must be . . . stolen from the note standing after the dot'; he notates the manner of execution by setting down two dots followed by a shortened note.[12] The quavers in this movement would then also be *inégales* and would coincide with the small note in the dotted rhythm as appropriate (Ex. 6.1).[13] In the Larghetto the differentiation of dotted rhythms from straight quavers might not preclude the introduc-

Ex. 6.2 Handel, *Ouverture* for two clarinets and horn, Andante allegro, bars 31–2

tion of a marginal element of *notes inégales* in the latter. The repeated halves of this movement offer the possibility of some modest embellishment.

The character of the final two movements implies a detached style of performance. The Andante allegro introduces triplets against duplets and raises the question of whether they should be synchronised. The slurred staccato in bars 31, 32 and 35 is a convention thought by Thurston Dart to convey performance of the quavers as written (Ex. 6.2).[14] Elsewhere, the balance of evidence suggests that the individual quavers in bars 14, 15, 26, 27, 31, 32, 36 and 37 might be aligned with the triplets which occur simultaneously. It is true that Agricola claimed that J. S. Bach taught his pupils to play clashing binary and ternary rhythms as notated, 'otherwise the difference between duple metre . . . and 3/8, 6/8, 9/8 and 12/8 would be eliminated'.[15] But context, style and tempo are important parameters for decision making in this area.

Handel's *Ouverture* may be modest in scope and dimensions, but it incorporates a wide variety of performance practice issues, posing some questions which cannot as yet be fully answered.

Johann Stamitz: Clarinet Concerto in B♭

Attribution and source

The Mannheim composer Johann Stamitz (1717–57) enjoyed a particular association with the clarinet during his year's stay in Paris from September 1754, when he conducted the orchestra of the wealthy arts patron A.-J.-J. de La Pouplinière. From this period must date his quartet for two B♭

clarinets and two E♭ horns included in Roeser's *Essai d'instruction* of 1764.[16] It is noted there that 'We played this piece in the presence of Mr Stamitz during his journey to Paris ...' Stamitz's Paris symphonies included clarinets on several occasions (see Rice, pp. 133, 154–5), often paired with horns. The title-page of the collection *La Melodia Germanica* (Paris, 1758), which comprises symphonies by Stamitz, Kohaut, Richter and Wagenseil, states that the music may be played with two oboes, flutes or violins in place of clarinets, thus implying a preference for the latter.[17] The clarinettists Gaspard Proksch and Simon Flieger played in the orchestra of La Pouplinière and took part in the première of Rameau's opera *Acante et Céphise* in 1753; they played in a Concert Spirituel under Stamitz two years later. Other clarinettists who worked with Stamitz at this time were François Reiffer and Jean Schieffer; they had taken part in the first performance of Rameau's *Zoroastre* in 1749.[18]

Johann's son Karl Stamitz (1745–1801) was a leading figure among the second generation of Mannheim orchestral composers, both prolific and cosmopolitan in style, a widely travelled performer and a major contributor to solo literature for the clarinet. Identification of his solo clarinet concertos has been inconsistent, though recent scholarship lists a total of ten, of which five were published between 1777 and 1793. All but one are scored for B♭ clarinet. Their idiomatic solo writing was subjected to close analysis in Helmut Boese's *Die Klarinette als Soloinstrument in der Musik der Mannheimer Schule* (Dresden, 1940).

The clarinet concerto widely attributed to Johann Stamitz was first brought to public attention in 1936 in an article by Peter Gradenwitz.[19] Importantly, its identification as a work of Johann rather than Karl is based on stylistic rather than documentary evidence, the mere ascription 'del Sig^n Stamitz' appearing in the set of manuscript parts in the Thurn and Taxis Court Library at Regensburg. In support of his attribution to Johann Stamitz, Gradenwitz drew attention to the concerto's heroic gestures, varied repetitions of material, use of thematic material and structural discipline. The degree of solo virtuosity is in fact greater than in most later Mannheim concertos, incorporating use of the low register and some very characteristic figuration, which (unlike some contemporary concertos) make the solo part entirely idiomatic for the clarinet and quite unsuitable for any other instrument. Leaps range over more than two octaves and there is also some high writing up to *e'''*, which resembles Molter's clarino-type writing.

Furthermore, Karl's work never includes repetition of subjects beginning on different beats of the bar, a practice surviving from an earlier period before the bar-line exerted such a strong influence. It is significant that the Adagio relies for its effect on florid gesture rather than the slow cantabile cultivated by later composers. The final Poco presto, whilst typically less demanding than the opening movement, incorporates wide-ranging gestures which show a real feeling for appropriate idiom.

Editions

Gradenwitz published an edition for Leeds Music Corporation (New York) in 1953. This scarcely conforms to today's ideals of performance practice; it is highly interventionist in terms of dynamics and phrasing, as well as incorporating some over-florid cadenzas. The curious omission of a single bar (184) in the finale is another serious shortcoming. Even more heavily laden with editorial accretions is Jacques Lancelot's 1982 version for Billaudot (Paris), which prescribes an under-articulated interpretation. In these circumstances the 1967 edition for Schott (Mainz) by Walter Lebermann emerges as the clear first choice. He leaves solo dynamics to the taste of the performer and his few suggested phrase markings are clearly differentiated from those of the composer. None the less, one might question his editorial decision to omit the clarinet from the tutti statements of the main theme at the beginning and end of the finale. Indeed, since the soloist must originally have played an important part in directing this concerto, some solo participation in the orchestral tuttis as a whole should perhaps be encouraged. On the other hand, it must be acknowledged (as with Mozart's Concerto) that clarinet involvement has a far greater effect on the orchestral tone-colour than is the case in solo works for such instruments as the violin or bassoon.[20]

Performance practice

Extremely few clarinets in B♭ or A survive from before about 1770. Some exist with three keys (the third being the e/b′ key, initially operated by Rth rather than L4) and a handful more with four keys (the fourth being either the a♭′/e♭″ key for R4 or, more rarely, the f♯/c♯″ key for L4, the latter

option typically French).[21] The earliest dated English instrument derives from 1770 and has five keys.[22] Several clarinets by distinguished makers after that date have fewer than five keys, but there are few five-keyed instruments which show evidence of being earlier than 1770. Thus if the concerto under discussion actually pre-dates the death of Johann Stamitz in 1757, it may have been intended for a three- or four-keyed clarinet. Though requiring some technical agility of the soloist, the only note which causes serious difficulty is the chalumeau b in bars 99–100 of the first movement. This note was also freely required by Karl Stamitz and Mozart, who may have envisaged half-holing from R1 at a time when this was a common practice on the oboe.

An absolute priority must be clearly to establish the character of each movement. In the opening Allegro moderato, much of the musical expression is achieved by means of dissonance and its resolution, for example in bar 2 of the solo (Ex. 6.3). All such dissonance needs emphasis, with a release and diminuendo at the resolution; this applies equally to the many accented appoggiaturas.[23] In keeping with the nature of the movement, longer note-values such as crotchets and quavers, should at no time be played legato (Ex. 6.4). Dynamics can be determined by means of the melodic contour and harmonic vocabulary, with echo effects introduced during repetitions in passage-work. The movement is at once highly expressive and virtuosic. As in the following Adagio, a modest cadenza is required; in both instances it is wise to heed Quantz's advice that such an improvisation should be playable in one breath.[24] The cantabile solo line of the Adagio again relies for its effect upon dissonance, the language of the slur and expressive long notes. The liveliness of the Poco presto is most readily reflected in a detached style of performance within a sparkling one-in-a bar; its flavour is arguably easier to achieve on a lighter-toned boxwood clarinet. Undoubtedly, this Stamitz concerto is a work where a modern legato approach allied to a limited variety of tongue-stroke strongly militates against the emergence of the

Ex. 6.4 Stamitz, Clarinet Concerto, Allegro moderato, bars 60–1 (*with performance suggestions*)

music's true character. Nor is it difficult to argue that the Boehm-system clarinet is altogether too heavy in tonal quality to execute the composer's intentions, insofar as they can be ascertained.

The horn parts listed in the title of the concerto do not survive, but as Gradenwitz deduces from analogous works, they were surely not indispensable. This piece therefore finds a place among a small and select group of solo clarinet works which can be played with the accompaniment of a string orchestra, though from a historical viewpoint the addition of a harpsichord continuo is essential.

Mozart : Clarinet Quintet K581

Genesis

Mozart noted in his own catalogue that the Clarinet Quintet was completed in Vienna on 29 September 1789; Anton Stadler gave the first performance in the Burgtheater on 22 December in a subscription concert of the Tonkünstler-Sozietät. On 9 April 1790 the work was performed again in the presence of Mozart and his friend Michael Puchberg at the house of Count Andreas Hadik. Stadler continued to play it long after Mozart's death and gave a performance as late as 5 July 1804 in a concert series organised by the celebrated violinist Ignaz Schuppanzigh.[25] The autographs of Mozart's Clarinet Quintet and Concerto are now lost and it is significant that on 31 May 1800 his widow Constanze wrote to the publisher André: 'For information about other works of this kind you should apply to the elder Stadler, the clarinettist, who used to possess the original manuscripts of several, and has copies of some trios for basset horn that are still unknown. Stadler declares that while he was in Germany his portmanteau was stolen, with these pieces in it. Others, however, assure me that the said portmanteau was pawned there for 73 ducats; but there were, I believe, instruments and other things in it as well.'[26]

Sources

The first edition was issued by André in 1802 as *Œuvre 108*, with the publisher's number 1602. Another early print was issued by Artaria & Co. in July 1802, plate no. 1536. A further edition by Sieber of Paris, *c.* 1812–22, plate no. 1679 is an arrangement for string quintet. Other arrangements included a version for piano quartet. An authoritative modern text, Series VIII/19/2 of the *Neue Mozart-Ausgabe*, is based on these sources and dates from 1956. Earlier editions by distinguished clarinettists such as Frederick Thurston (London, 1941) are more interventionist in terms of articulation and dynamics, areas within which most performers will nowadays prefer to make informed choices for themselves.

Performance practice

It now seems certain that Mozart's Quintet was originally intended for Stadler's newly built basset clarinet, an instrument discussed in detail in Chapter 7. Early editions of the Quintet, like those of the Concerto, were in effect transcriptions for normal clarinet. The basset clarinet had a range extended by four semitones to notated low *c* (sounding *a* on the A clarinet), a feature borrowed from the closely related basset horn. Jiří Kratochvíl played the Quintet on a specially reconstructed instrument at the International Mozart Conference in Prague in 1956 and subsequently published a series of articles on the subject.[27]

Most boxwood re-creations of the basset clarinet have simply an extended tube (as with Boehm-system instruments) or a design scaled down from surviving eighteenth-century basset horns.[28] In 1801 Friedrich Bertuch noted that Stadler's clarinet did not run straight down to the bell but that about the last quarter of its length was fitted with a transverse pipe, from which a projecting bell flared out further.[29] This description matches an engraving found by Pamela Poulin in surviving programmes from Stadler's 1794 concerts in Riga, where the design incorporates curved barrel, straight tube cul-

Ex. 6.5 Mozart, Clarinet Quintet, Allegro, bars 99–102

minating in a 90° angle and bulb bell. A reconstructed instrument based on the sketch is illustrated in Lawson, *Mozart: Clarinet Concerto*, p. 47. Further corroboration for this model comes from an incomplete letter dated 2 May 1795 from Stadler to Daniel Schütte, music director of the theatre at Bremen, arranging performances there and commissioning from the maker Tietzel 'eine neue Art Clarinette d'amour' ('a new type of *clarinette d'amour*') of his own specification.[30]

Reconstruction of the text is a less radical affair than with the Concerto, though it has not been attempted in any modern edition, including the *Neue Mozart-Ausgabe*. As long ago as 1948 George Dazeley drew attention to several passages which he suspected had been altered from an original basset version, such as bars 41, 99–110, 114, 185, 187, 196–7 in the first movement; bars 9 and 43 in Trio 2 of the Menuetto; in the finale, bars 3, 7, 13, 14 in variation 1: bars 8 and 16 in variations 2 and 3: bars 1, 3, 13 and 16 in variation 4: and bar 36 in the coda.[31] Of these, the arpeggios at 1/99–110 are most problematic; one possible reconstruction is given in *Early Music*, 15 (1987), p. 491 and in Ex. 6.5 Bar 100 is the only context in the Quintet where a basset c♯ may have been required, and the question remains whether Stadler's basset clarinet in A originally was extended only to c, d and e♭, notes demanded of the basset *horn* in Mozart's Serenade K361.

As noted elsewhere in this book, timing and tempo flexibility are areas where the aesthetic still apparent in early twentieth-century recordings has all but disappeared. Of course, there were many admonitions to keep strict time during the eighteenth and nineteenth centuries, because the ability to keep a steady beat was difficult to acquire and a mark of professionalism.

C. P. E. Bach and a host of other writers were in fact warning against tempo modifications which occurred unintentionally. Relevant to an emphasis on the darker elements in the Clarinet Quintet are the following remarks by the pianist Daniel Gottlob Türk, encouraging a greater degree of freedom: 'A tenderly, moving passage between two lively, fiery ideas . . . can be played somewhat hesitatingly; only in this case one does not take the tempo gradually slower, but *immediately* a little (however only a *little*) slower.'[32] The second subject at bars 42 and 148 of the first movement and variation 3 of the finale are among contexts for this treatment, although underlining the whole issue is the fact that we are bound to interpret eighteenth-century evidence from the viewpoint of our own musical taste, which has tended to become less flexible and improvisatory than in earlier times. We are all too easily satisfied with a self-effacing reading of the score, rather than an intuitive response to the code contained within the musical notation itself. As for Mozart's tempo markings, the Larghetto of the second movement is probably a quicker indication than the Adagio in his Clarinet Concerto. As we observed in Chapter 5, Quantz clearly distinguishes these categories and further points out that whilst every marking has an individual meaning it refers more to the dominant passions in each piece than to the tempo proper.[33] One might add further that in recognising the strong operatic links with Mozart's clarinet music, the player should choose tempi for slower movements which are vocally conceived and therefore not too pedestrian.

The principal area of performance practice in Mozart remains the formulation of an articulated, well-modulated sense of melodic inflection. The range of tongue strokes expected by the flautist Quantz is a salutary reminder of the attention paid to this subject during the eighteenth century. The degree of separation must be varied according to context and phrase-structure. Stylistically aware playing must also take account of other elements outlined in Chapter 5, including the hierarchy of the bar, melodic contour, phrasing and the role of dissonance and its resolution. An example early in the first movement is the clarinet's dissonance with the violins on the minim beats at bar 20 (Ex. 6.6). The second subject (violin 1, bars 42–8: clarinet, bars 49–62) relies for much of its effect on written-out appoggiaturas at bars 44, 46 and so on, which each demand emphasis and immediate shading (Ex. 6.7). The syncopated effect in the clarinet's recapitulation of this second

Ex. 6.6 Mozart, Clarinet Quintet, Allegro, bars 19–20

Ex. 6.7 Mozart, Clarinet Quintet, Allegro, bars 49–51

Ex. 6.8 Mozart, Clarinet Quintet, Allegro, bars 155–7

subject (bars 155ff.) needs to be emphasised by means of the small-scale slurs (Ex. 6.8). Although the sum of the evidence is ambiguous, trills (other than the chain at 1/182–4) might begin with a stressed upper note and with some degree of elegant acceleration.

Attention to dissonance and the language of the slur remains important in the Larghetto. Attention to the hierarchy of the bar suggests avoidance of stresses on weak beats, for example the final quavers of bars such as 3 and 5. An important further question arises whether to ornament the return of the opening at bar 51. Is this in fact the type of context described by Türk as being so communicative and speaking directly to the heart of the listener that no 'false glitter' is appropriate ? Türk proceeds to state that only those passages should be varied which would otherwise not be interesting enough. Even if we are persuaded that Stadler might have indulged in some decoration, our own personal conviction as performers is surely important

Ex. 6.9 Mozart, Clarinet Quintet, Menuetto, bars 1–8

here. The many returns of the opening strain of the Menuetto might also be possible candidates for some elaboration (Ex. 6.9). In the finale, we may note again the paired notes in variation 1 and the continuous semiquavers in variation 4, where the articulation must have been left to Stadler's judgement. The violin 1 response here has a two-slurred, two-articulated pattern. The wedge-shaped staccato in variation 3 (and also in the Larghetto, violin 1, bars 22, 72) has proved ambiguous but almost certainly implies a degree of emphasis which counteracts the hierarchy of the bar. In support of this, Ozi's contemporary bassoon tutor proposes a harder tongue stroke for the wedge. We may note finally that some modest embellishment is invited at the fermata immediately before the coda.

A final question remains the degree to which a piece such as Mozart's Clarinet Quintet was originally projected, given that early performances were indeed true chamber music overheard by a select audience. Stadler's tone was clearly highly seductive, and the extent to which a contemporary venue matches eighteenth-century conditions might well determine one's approach here. A concluding word on performing ambience may be left with Stadler himself, who wrote that there was no accounting for the particular mood of an audience on a given evening:

> For example, yesterday the cards were unfavourable for this lady [in the audience], this young gentleman has been jilted by his sweetheart, this official was passed over in advancement . . . the banker has won only 99 per cent [interest], the malicious denouncer has failed to catch his prey, the junior officer who has served only twenty-four hours is not already at least a brigadier-general; [and] in such a mood in a large part does the public condemn the author, composer, actor and performing artists.[34]

Weber Clarinet Concerto No. 2 in E♭ Op. 74

Genesis and reception

There have been many celebrated associations of composers and clarinettists, of which the relationship between Carl Maria von Weber and Heinrich Baermann was especially fruitful. In 1811 Weber arrived in Munich, where Baermann was principal clarinet of the court orchestra, and quickly wrote the Concertino for him. After his magnificent performance on April 5, Weber's two clarinet concertos were commissioned by the King of Bavaria. Weber completed the First Concerto in May of that year and began the Second during the following month. Baermann premièred the latter at a public concert given by the court tenor Georg Weixelbaum on 25 November. In his diary Weber described the 'frantic applause owing to Baermann's godlike playing'. Details of the clarinettist's career have been recounted by Pamela Weston, including various appreciations of his playing. For example, in Vienna during 1812 Prince Lobkowitz declared that Baermann's playing was 'so melodious that singers would do well to find out his secrets of cantabile'. Weston observes that he had an innate sense of style and his interpretations were always well formed.

> His adagios had the power to move audiences to tears. Finger dexterity he had too, but it always came second to the musical interpretation. Schilling says he was 'a thorough artist in temperament and a man of refined taste'. Carl [Baermann] says of his father that he played 'so nobly, so soulfully and earnestly' and 'when he played fast and daring pieces of music, I have nowhere heard an artist who played with such fine shades of nuances'. His dear friend Weber called him a 'truly great artist and wonderful man', and Mendelssohn wrote to the pianist Kohlreif: 'He is one of the best musicians I know; one of those who carry everyone along with them, and who feel the true life and fire of music, and to whom music has become speech.'[35]

Another early exponent of Weber's Second Concerto was Spohr's clarinettist Simon Hermstedt, who played it at concerts in Prague on 10 and 17 February 1815.[36] The two clarinettists were often compared, and Weber wrote in his diary:

Hermstedt played twice very beautifully. A thick, almost stuffy tone. Surmounts tremendous difficulties, sometimes completely against the nature of the instrument, but not always well. Also pleasing delivery. Has many strings to his bow, which is all to the good. But lacks the uniform quality of tone which Baermann has between the high and low notes, and his heavenly tasteful delivery.[37]

Sources

A delicate problem for an historically aware performance is the relationship between Weber's original composition and the additions variously made by Heinrich Baermann and by his son Carl. A readily available modern text which attempts to differentiate these contributions is the Breitkopf & Härtel score (no. 4922), edited by Günther Hausswald. The piano reduction for Fentone (F440) by Pamela Weston gives Weber's original text as well as her edited version, providing an appropriate context for the performer's own initiative.

Weber's autograph in the possession of the composer's family is discussed in some detail by Hausswald, for whom it was the principal source. The score contains numerous pencillings by Weber's biographer Friedrich Wilhelm Jähns (1809–88), indicating details of Baermann's interpretation of dynamics, phrasing and tempo markings. These notes derive from another autograph score formerly in the possession of Carl Baermann, which has disappeared since the time of Jähns. They are all clearly tabulated in Hausswald's *Revisionsbericht* in the preface to his edition. Other less important sources are a copy of the autograph by Jähns dated August 1869 surviving in Berlin, and a further contemporary copy in Dresden by the composer Julius Rietz (1812–77). The Berlin firm of Schlesinger was the first to publish a piano reduction (together with orchestral parts), which claimed to include interpretative detail not included in the autograph, much of which derived from Carl Baermann. But it was the later revised practical edition (still widely available) by a third generation of Baermanns (Carl, 1839–1913) which led to particular confusion as to the original detail of Weber's solo part. The Carl Baermann edition is much more ornate than Weber's original, and not just as a result of added dynamics and phrasing. Melodic contours are sometimes embellished, as at bars 165–6 of the first movement (Ex.

Ex. 6.10 Weber, Clarinet Concerto No. 2, Allegro, bars 165–7

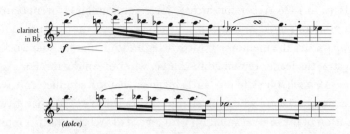

Ex. 6.11 Weber, Clarinet Concerto No. 2, Alla polacca, bars 59 and 65

6.10) and bars 59 and 65 of the finale (Ex. 6.11). Equally importantly, this type of later edition tends to mask the language of the slur, which continued to characterise music of Weber's period; indications here should be considered critically, with reference to earlier sources.

It is highly significant that Heinrich Baermann's timings for each movement were respectively 10, 8 and 8½ minutes. Modern averages are around 8½–9, 7 and 6–6½ minutes, indicating that tempi have increased overall, particularly in the finale.[38] Whatever the parameters for modern performance, it seems clear that the opportunity for expressive nuance cannot afford to be sacrificed for the sake of mere technical exhibitionism.

Interpretation

The premières of Weber's clarinet concertos were given at a time when orchestras were still being directed in a variety of ways. In the opera house Weber changed performance practice in this respect, assuming the responsibilities of baton conductor from the violinist-concertmaster, as reported by Berlioz in relation to the Dresden Court Theatre in 1818.[39] Similarly, in 1826 Weber conducted *Oberon* at London's Covent Garden 'at the conductor's desk', and later conducted in concert the overture to *Ruler of the Spirits*. But the memoirs of Moscheles indicate that for solo works with orchestra, the leader remained in charge, without conductor. For example, during Mendelssohn's tenure in Leipzig as (baton) conductor, it was the concertmaster David who took charge of solo works.[40] This may give some indication of the orginal situation with regard to Weber's clarinet music.

The use of period instruments in Weber's clarinet concertos reveals an especially subtle tonal palette, considerably enhancing the effect of his extraordinarily imaginative orchestration. The more gentle, rounded sound of the boxwood clarinet makes a discreet blend with the strings, enabling it to melt into the texture. The orchestral wind section is potentially more vivid in colour, contributing to Weber's continuously changing sound-world. These factors can help to explain the excitement felt by early audiences and the music's instant success. The extreme difficulty of the solo part and inherent sense of danger was another important element, an exhilarating aspect greatly reduced by the technical developments of later instruments. Baermann's personality and his ability to move an audience attracted Weber's attention and any performance needs to take account of this, moving well beyond mere establishment of the musical text.

The balance of primary evidence suggests that a considerable degree of tempo flexibility would have been applied during Weber's lifetime. On the other hand, there is no reason to suppose that a classically articulated style of performance had been abandoned. Within each movement Weber's use of longer phrase marks of two to four bars to denote legato should in no way discourage such an overall approach, even taking into account the extension to nine bars at the recapitulation in the Romanza (bars 74–82).[41] Where material occurs twice, Weber does not give the required phrasing on each occasion, as can be seen in the second subject of the first movement, where bars 103–4 acquire a phrase mark when repeated at bars 111–12. Elsewhere, the composer's own text leaves much articulation to the individual performer, especially in the faster passage-work. Here, the much-used two-slurred, two-tongued approach can be appropriate, whilst the contour of the semiquaver lines can sometimes suggest other patterns. Legato passage-work is probably best slurred in crotchet (or at most minim) beats, with

Ex. 6.12 Weber, Clarinet Concerto No. 2, Allegro, bars 50–1 (*with performance suggestions*)

fresh articulation at the beginning of each bar. Meanwhile, longer note-values (as in the Concerto's first solo entry, Ex. 6.12) need always to be detached and alive in spirit; the character of faster movements can easily be diluted by sustained notes which are too long and lacking in nuance.

Brahms: Clarinet Trio Op. 114

Reception

Brahms's Clarinet Trio was premièred on 12 December 1891 by Richard Mühlfeld and Brahms, together with the cellist of the Joachim Quartet, Robert Hausmann.[42] Recently there has been much interest in attempting to recreate his intimate sound-world, both in orchestral and chamber music. Brahms apparently preferred the clarinet and piano medium to that with strings, finding a better blend from the combination. The composer himself rated his Trio as highly as the Clarinet Quintet, but it was not as well received and has continued to attract criticism ever since. Among reviewers there has been no unanimity even as to its essential character. But several of Brahms's friends seem actually to have preferred the Trio, not least Eusebius Mandyczewski, who commented that its effect was as if the instruments were in love with one another. More recently, Malcolm MacDonald has observed that

> the work's emotional range is much wider than the Quintet, and far less amenable to merely comfortable interpretations. Standing at the very end of his long line of concerted chamber music with piano, it exhibits all the resource and subtlety of his late style, further stimulated by the contrasting characters of the three instruments, which permit little of the Quintet's blended sonority.[43]

Sources

The two principal sources are Brahms's autograph and his personal copy of the work in the edition published by Simrock in 1892 (plate no. 9709), which contains corrections in his own hand. At a number of points, particularly at the close of the first movement, the autograph differs considerably from the first edition, which presumably incorporates alterations subsequently made by Brahms.[44] An Urtext such as the Henle Edition (1979) by Monica Steegman tabulates the divergences and is at the same time reliable in terms of dynamics and articulation.

Richard Mühlfeld

At the end of his life Brahms considered that the art of clarinet playing had been deteriorating and that orchestral players in Vienna and elsewhere sounded fairly good, but gave no real pleasure as soloists. Mühlfeld proved a glorious exception, inspiring Brahms on boxwood Baermann-system clarinets designed around 1860 and purchased by him c. 1875. Their softer-edged sound reflects the intimate sound-world of the Meiningen orchestra, with its relatively modest complement of players. As we have noted already, Mühlfeld's surviving instruments at the Stadtmuseum at Meiningen suggest that he played at a pitch close to the modern level of a' = 440. When these clarinets were recently examined, they were found to have excellent intonation; furthermore, 'the overall effect is a most beautiful warm tone, just what one would hope to discover at the source of Brahms's inspiration'.[45] There is some evidence that Mühlfeld (who began life as a violinist) employed a strong vibrato and that on the clarinet this was unusual. In 1863 Moritz Hauptmann had claimed that a wind note with vibrato was as impossible as a vibrated harmonic. This opinion was contradicted by Arrey von Dommer in 1865, who reckoned that vibrato was effective on both the flute and the oboe.[46]

Brahms called Mühlfeld the nightingale of the orchestra, whilst Liszt compared his playing to the sensation of biting into a ripe peach. Clara Schumann described his playing as at once delicate, warm and unaffected, at the same time showing the most perfect technique and command of the instrument. There is considerable evidence that Mühlfeld's tone and delivery differed markedly from the British tradition. George Bernard Shaw found the sound rich, but not so pure as that of Henry Lazarus, England's foremost player at the time of Mühlfeld's first visits. The English clarinettist George Garside (himself renowned for a full, rich, golden sound) heard him as a boy and reported that Mühlfeld was a fine technician, 'but his tone was comic'. In 1916 Oscar Street praised his phrasing, but reckoned that his tone and execution left much to be desired. Vaughan Williams felt that where Mühlfeld played with the tone and fire of a violinist, Charles Draper brought out the true quality of the clarinet. There is more to these criticisms than mere British chauvinism. Mühlfeld was clearly a highly individual player and thus likely to divide opinion even on his own territory. Friedrich Buxbaum, who had been cellist in the Rosé Quartet and had played the Trio with Mühlfeld during Brahms's lifetime, commented in 1940 that there were plenty of better clarinettists in Vienna in the 1890s.[47]

Sonority

The cellist Hausmann is reported to have used rather more vibrato than his violinist colleague Joachim, who recommended its use only as an expressive device. Furthermore, early recordings show that the portamento, a conspicuous slide between positions, served to shape string melodies by calling attention to certain structurally important pitches.[48] The use of gut for the cello strings produces what one writer has described as a tone 'richer in strong upper overtones, more complex and full than that of steel strings'.[49] The introduction of the cello endpin around 1860 offered the instrument a greater security, mobility and resonance, though it was not adopted by Hausmann. But it was employed by other cellists who played with Mühlfeld, such as Karl Piening of the Wendling Quartet.[50]

Around 1869 Brahms was presented with a seven-octave Streicher piano by the builder, and this was the instrument he was using during the 1890s.

> Although Streicher now employed heavier hammers with inner coverings of felt, the outer layer remained leather. The wooden bracing was stouter than that on instruments built before the middle of the century, though reinforced by only two longitudinal iron bars rather than the six that were now standard on Erards.[51]

The characteristic quick decay and registral variety commonly found among late nineteenth-century Viennese pianos was maintained.

In keeping with the characteristics of cello and piano, Mühlfeld's clarinets belonged to a tradition which readily relates back to the five-keyed instruments of Mozart's day. Each note retains its own individual personality, matching the lesser tension of the other two instruments by comparison with their modern counterparts. The fine resonance of the Baermann system derives from the relatively few tone-holes in relation to the number of alternative touch-pieces. Only recently has a theoretical understanding been gained of the disadvantage of designing an instrument with an excessive number of tone-holes.[52]

Tempo flexibility, articulation and nuance

Aside from tonal elements, the principal stylistic areas for a study of Brahms's performance practice are tempo flexibility, articulation and nuance. All these must have been important interpretative parameters when the Trio was first performed; after all, it was principally as an artist that Mühlfeld was admired. As we have already noted, his performances were given at a time when musical tempo was considerably more flexible than it is today, and fluctuations in the surface rhythm of individual passages as well as basic pulse for longer passages were common. Brahms himself made the oft-quoted remark that tempo flexibility should be applied 'con discrezione', a comment which nowadays certainly needs to be read in terms of the prevailing aesthetic. On the metronome, Brahms made it clear that tempo in his music could not be constant. Recorded evidence from the early twentieth century suggests that individual subjects in sonata form were assigned their own tempi, connected by transitional passages; unstable areas in the development and coda often featured accelerating tempi to heighten tension and drama where appropriate. Brahms's more general advice to at least one player is revealing; 'Do it how you like, but make it beautiful.' This is a telling remark in the context of a tradition dating back at least as far as Maczewski's article in *Grove 1* (1879), which emphasised the intellectual (rather than technical) qualities in his playing. Most clarinettists will cherish the story of Brahms's attendance at a rehearsal of his Clarinet Quintet, at which he was so touched that tears came to his eyes. To cover his emotion he marched across the room, closed the first violin part and growled, 'Stop that terrible music !'[53]

Clara Schumann's pupil Fanny Davies (1861–1934), who premièred the

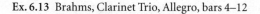

Ex. 6.13 Brahms, Clarinet Trio, Allegro, bars 4–12

piano parts of Brahms's clarinet works in England (the composer being unwilling to travel), left an important reminiscence of Brahms's own playing at the end of Tovey's article on Brahms in *Cobbett's Cyclopaedic Survey of Chamber Music* (Oxford, 1929). She reports that his manner of interpretation was free, very elastic and expansive, but with a balance of fundamental and surface rhythms. He listened intently to inner harmonies, laying great stress on good basses. His economical marks of expression were intended to convey the inner musical meaning. The sign <> often occurred when he wished to express great sincerity and warmth, applied not only to tone but also to rhythm. He would linger not on one note alone, but on a whole idea, as if unable to tear himself away from its beauty. He would prefer to lengthen a bar or phrase rather than spoil it by making up the time into a metronomic bar. We have already noted in previous chapters of this book that the playing of Brahms's violinist friend Joachim was similarly flexible, if not indeed improvisatory.

Especially important to the overall characterisation of Brahms's music are his small-scale markings relating to articulation. In the previous chapter we noted that Brahms regarded the shortening of the second of a pair of notes as obligatory, an important feature of the opening of the Trio, for example in bars 18 and 20. In Chapter 2 we also discussed the meaning of Brahms's rhetorical notation and the fact that the modern performer's stereotype of long uninterrupted phrases runs counter to the practice of musicians trained during his lifetime. The separation of melodic and motivic units reveals his penchant for composing continually developing variations. Such interpretation lends rhetorical variety to individual themes and heightened dramatic contrasts to whole movements, as shown by the language of the slur in Ex.

Ex. 6.14 Brahms, Clarinet Trio, Allegro [finale], bars 85–92

6.13 and Ex. 6.14. Further expressive potential and emotional qualities will thus be revealed in Brahms's music, when coupled to emphases relating to the hierarchy of the bar, dissonance and its resolution and the influence of melodic contour. For this kind of articulated practice we have the evidence of early recordings as well as explicit descriptions. Joseph Bloch of the Budapest Conservatory wrote in 1903: 'The main point of phrasing is to make the work more understandable to the listeners. Phrasing results in the separation of individual parts, from which one can clearly recognise and distinguish the melodic members which have developed out of a pre-existent motive from those which are totally new.'[54]

7   Related family members

Introduction

No other instrument can lay claim to quite such a large and diverse family as the clarinet and even the orchestral player's basic equipment of a *pair* of instruments serves to distinguish him from other instrumentalists. The Boehm-system clarinet exists in as many as twenty-five different types and sizes. The tiniest is the scarcely known clarinet in high C, more than an octave higher than the instruments in common use; in increasing order of size there are then piccolo, sopranino, soprano, alto and bass clarinets ranging down to the B♭ contrabass. Least familiar are perhaps those clarinets smaller in size than the E♭, though there have also been some shadowy larger representatives, such as the *clarinettes d'amour* in A♭ and G (pitched just below the normal A clarinet) from the latter half of the eighteenth century.

Special projects: high clarinets

The byways of clarinet repertory involve a variety of rare instruments. For example, the stage band in Verdi's *La traviata* finds a rare appearance of the tiny A♭ clarinet in mainstream art music. A solo project involving the closely related clarinet in high G might be a recreation of the so-called *Schrammelquartett*, an ensemble much admired by Richard Strauss, Brahms and Hans Richter. Active in the 1880s, this group consisted of two violins (the Schrammel brothers), bass guitar and G clarinet. It was recreated in the mid-1960s, following discovery of the autographs of the waltzes and polkas which formed its core repertory. The small clarinet in G was nicknamed (in Viennese slang) 'picksüßes Hölzl', or 'fabulous matchstick'. Other *Schrammel* groups have since been formed, and late-nineteenth-century German-system ten-keyed G clarinets have appeared in the catalogue of at least one modern maker.

Of other high clarinets, the D has the longest pedigree (with baroque repertory by Handel, Molter and others), but numerous original E♭ clarinets survive, with as few as five brass keys. For the earliest orchestral contexts, such as the *Symphonie Fantastique* by Berlioz, a thirteen-keyed model is probably appropriate. After 1845, when Wagner used the D clarinet in *Tannhäuser*, both instruments were increasingly used in German and Austrian orchestral music. Surviving specimens indicate that the fingering systems of the B♭ and A clarinets were reproduced by manufacturers of the smaller instruments.

Low clarinets

The role in musical history of the *clarinette d'amour* remains something of an enigma, which is not solved merely by examination of surviving specimens. The instrument has been the subject of some discussion in print.[1] The unusual *clarinette d'amour* in D appears in J. C. Bach's overture to *Temistocle*, whilst three trios formerly attributed to Haydn have the instrument pitched in B♭.

Bass clarinets (an octave below the soprano in B♭ or C) were made from the 1770s onwards. The majority of early examples (before 1820) were extended to written low C, and several models were devised in bassoon form, probably for use in military bands. It has been suggested that the American George Catlin was the most prolific maker of early bass clarinets,[2] and that it was in the 1820s that alto and bass clarinets emerged with the same range as the normal clarinet. Their design was radically improved by Adolphe Sax, who enlarged the bore and the toneholes, redesigned the keywork and enlarged the mouthpiece. The B♭ bass clarinet became a member of the orchestra from the mid nineteenth century and instruments in A were also used, at least in areas under German influence. The first major orchestral bass clarinet solo occurs in Meyerbeer's *Les Huguenots*, whilst a rare appearance of the bass clarinet in C is contained in Liszt's symphonic poem *Mazeppa*. Old bass clarinets survive in a variety of systems (depicted in clarinet literature such as Kroll and Rendall) and usually descend to low e or e♭. This latter was the norm until the early 1960s, though many significant works had already demanded a compass to c, such as Stravinsky's *Petrouchka* and Prokofiev's *Romeo and Juliet*.

Before testing an original bass clarinet, its pitch should be clearly established. Many of the other criteria recommended for choosing a modern instrument apply, in terms of response and tuning.[3]

Basset horn, basset clarinet

Mozart's central position in the history of the clarinet ensures that the period player will inevitably take a keen interest in the basset instruments. His Serenade K361 and the Requiem are now regularly performed on period instruments, but Mozart's idiomatic engagement with the basset horn also extends to a range of smaller pieces.[4] Of these, the Adagio K411 for two clarinets and three basset horns and the twenty-five pieces K439b for a trio of basset horns are small-scale works of unsurpassed quality.

The early history of the basset horn was one of rapid development. The first types, with sickle-shaped tube modelled on the oboe da caccia, borrowed the box or *Buch* just above its bell from instruments such as the rackett to achieve an extension down from written e to the tonic c. Neither the simplest instruments with four to six keys (probably *c.* 1760 and equivalent in development to the three-keyed clarinet) nor some instruments by the supposed inventors A. and M. Mayrhofer are furnished with any intervening notes.[5] A considerable attempt to clarify the complexities of basset horn history has been made by Nicholas Shackleton in his article 'The earliest basset horns' in *The Galpin Society Journal*, 40 (1987).

The classical basset horn became established in the 1780s and is described in H. C. Koch's *Musikalisches Lexicon* of 1802. The sickle shape was replaced by the more readily constructed design of two limbs joined at an angle by a knee. This type has been widely illustrated in the literature and has been widely copied by modern makers, often from Viennese models by makers such as Lotz and Griesbacher. Surviving specimens testify to the provision of a key for d at this time, though even as late as 1810–11 the somewhat conservative Joseph Fröhlich remarked that this note was not always present. Its addition may well constitute the improvement of 1782 attributed by C. F. Cramer to Theodor Lotz.[6] This Pressburg (Bratislava) maker was to become a seminal figure in the musical relationship of Mozart and Stadler. Eight-keyed basset horns were constructed in the 1780s and continued to be described much later, for example in G. Schilling's *Universal-Lexicon der Tonkunst* of 1840.[7]

In 1796 the brothers Anton and Johann Stadler were described as 'accomplished artists both on the ordinary clarinet and also on the basset clarinet, on which difficult instrument they have perfected control of tone-production, nuance, expression and facility'.[8] This is probably a reference to the basset horn, whose relatively narrow bore made it especially difficult to play. Similar terminology was used by Gottfried Weber in 1822 and recurs in still later sources. Albrechtsberger's attribution to the Stadler brothers of the addition of low c♯ and d♯ has some definite basis, even though surviving basset horns of the period have only c and d keys. Whether or not both chromatic notes became available at once, Mozart's attitude to the improvement at first shows restraint; the second basset horn part of the Serenade K361 has but a single passage requiring d and e♭ and but one instance of c. Shackleton has observed that on the eighteenth-century design of a flat *Buch* even the provision of d is not accomplished without difficulty because the hole to be covered is far off the line of the lever controlling it. It is just possible to add a close-standing key to provide low e♭, of which there are examples on later instruments of this design dating from 1800–20. But c♯ must also have been available to Stadler, as witnessed by Albrechtsberger's remarks; indeed, the note is required in the lowest basset horn part of Mozart's *Notturno* K436.[9]

Although the basset horns made by Lotz for the Stadlers must have been furnished with a flat *Buch*, other makers were manufacturing instruments of other designs well before the end of the century, in which the three bores in the box were in a triangle rather than beside each other in a flat box. Such makers include Grundmann and August Grenser in Dresden, Doleisch in Prague and Kirst in Potsdam. It is significant that Doleisch added an e♭ mechanism before 1800, an easier operation where the box was triangular. The earliest known basset horns to incorporate c♯ (in a triangular *Buch*) were made by Heinrich Grenser (and later by Grenser and Wiesner) and now form part of collections in Zurich, Basel, Ann Arbor and Boston. These instruments, however, date from twenty years or so after Mozart's death; their greater power and fully chromatic basset register render them suitable for Mendelssohn's *Konzertstücke* Opp. 113 and 114. Later nineteenth-century basset horns in a wide variety of designs are illustrated within the clarinet literature. The many parts written by Richard Strauss must have been played initially on German-system instruments. Among modern French manufacturers there is no real consensus as to what the basset horn should be, and in particular whether the relatively narrow bore should be retained.

Backofen, who also composed extensively for the basset horn, noted a similarity of tone and construction to the *Waldhorn*, presumably suggested by the metal bell. He claims that the finest basset horns were manufactured in Vienna, whilst noting that even their intonation needed to be corrected by applying wax to the tone-holes. Significantly, he regrets the lack of a groove in the bore to catch excess water which at present gets into the tone-holes and even the keys. Because the basset horn is a fairly heavy instrument, it is customary to attach a strap from the lower joint to a button on the player's coat, as happens with the bassoon. As noted in chapter 4, he remarks that reed-below players hold the instrument on the right-hand side, like the bassoon, whereas reed-above players put their right foot forward somewhat and rest the bell on the thigh. There are even players who, in order to find a stable position for the instrument, grip the narrow part of the bell between both thighs, though this makes for an extremely unhappy and wooden spectacle. Backofen recommends an oval shape for the bell, which enables it easily to be rested against one thigh, without any loss of tone-quality.

Recent performances on early basset horns or copies have helped to illuminate Mozart's fascination with the instrument, since its extraordinary acoustical make-up produces a sound which can truly be described as otherworldly; it is certainly one of the classical wind instruments which seems furthest removed from its modern counterpart. The basset horn's technical difficulty, perceived by a number of contemporary writers, remains evident today. The natural unevenness of scale is emphasised by the veiled quality of the cross-fingered notes and the instrument can be difficult to control. However, it is clear both from old basset horns and from good modern copies that tuning can be at least as accurate as on the modern Boehm system. None the less, certain passages in both basset horn parts of the Serenade K361 need creative handling in terms of fingering and embouchure and there can be no assumption that fingerings in the two principal registers will be identical.[10]

The basset clarinet is now in regular use for performances of Mozart's Quintet and Concerto on both modern and period instruments. Its first documentation occurs in a programme for a concert at the Vienna

Hoftheater on 20 February 1788.[11] It announces that 'Herr Stadler the elder
. . . will play a concerto on the *Bass-Klarinet* and a variation on the *Bass-Klarinet*, an instrument of new invention and manufacture of the court
instrument maker Theodor Loz [*sic*]; this instrument has two more tones
than the normal clarinet.' Stadler's instrument has become known in recent
times as the basset clarinet, a term coined by Jiří Kratochvíl to reflect its
kinship with the basset horn and to distinguish it from the bass clarinet. It
seems reasonable to assume that the special clarinet referred to in 1788 had a
diatonic extension of c and d, by analogy with the basset horn in normal use.
It was probably pitched in Bb. Backofen's tutor (*c*. 1803) shows awareness of
such an instrument: 'Another more recent and excellent invention is this,
that clarinets with d and c are now being made in Vienna; this greatly
improves the clarinet, because in addition to the great advantage which low
c brings, which until now it missed so much in its favourite key of C, it now
has three complete octaves, in which every clarinettist can play easily.'[12]

It seems certain that Stadler played basset clarinets to the exclusion of
normal clarinets from at least 1788 and that his own solo and duet compositions for clarinet would have been played on the extended instrument.
Cadenzas in Stadler's hand for a concerto probably by Joseph Michl are
scored for basset clarinet, as are vocal works by Paer and by Süssmayr. The
Lotz basset clarinet must also be associated with Mozart's Quintet fragment
K516c in Bb, ninety-three bars of a movement which, in 1828, Georg von
Nissen believed to have been originally complete.[13] Basset notes occur only
from bar 55, d then occurring seven times, occasioning notation in the bass
clef an octave below pitch, as in Mozart's basset horn writing. Robert Levin
was among those to reconstruct the movement and suggested that the
missing portion of K516c must have contained some examples of low c.[14]
The second clarinet part to Ferrando's aria 'Ah lo veggio' from *Così fan tutte*
also descends to c on a total of seven occasions.

A fully chromatic basset clarinet is mentioned for the first time in the
Berlin *Musikalische Korrespondenz* of 1790, which stated that Stadler had
'improved the instrument and added notes at the bottom, so that e is no
longer the lowest note, but rather the c below this. He also takes the intervening c♯ and d♯ with amazing ease.' A date of 1790 for these developments is
also suggested by Gerber's *Lexicon*. Lotz died in 1792 and credit for the new
instrument was henceforth claimed by Stadler. This more elaborate basset

Fig. 7.1 F. X. Süssmayr, Concerto in D for basset clarinet, autograph sketch, bars 112–25

clarinet must have been pitched in A. The various designs of basset clarinet described in the Mozart case study in the preceding chapter all have some historical basis; ease of provision of the chromatic basset mechanism (for which there is scant historical evidence) varies from one design to another. There is also some debate as to which type offers the most advantageous tone-quality, especially for the lowest notes. Surviving basset clarinets (as well as clarinets and basset horns relevant in design and provenance to a study of Mozart) have recently been tabulated and described in some detail.[15] During his Baltic tour, Stadler gave a concert in Riga on 5 March 1794 at which Mozart's Concerto was performed and also a Concerto in D by Süssmayr. Sketches for the latter are extant in the British Library and show that (unlike Mozart) Süssmayr was willing to utilise the basset clarinet's widely advertised four-octave range (Fig. 7.1).

A number of aspects of reconstructing Mozart's Clarinet Concerto have recently been subject to scrutiny, notably the establishment of his original text for basset clarinet.[16] Many areas of performance practice are involved, including articulation, nuance, tempo flexibility, ornamentation and improvistaion. The work must originally have been directed by the soloist, with some assistance from the Concertmaster. String forces may have been reduced during solo passages. A more controversial issue remains the continued participation of a keyboard player in Viennese instrumental repertoire of this period.[17] Re-creation of the Concerto on period instruments is indeed an elusive undertaking, though undoubtedly a highly rewarding experience.

Notes

1 The early clarinet in context

1 J. Fröhlich, *Vollständige theoretisch-praktische Musikschule* (Bonn, 1810–11), p. 15

2 J. J. Quantz, *Versuch einer Anweisung die Flöte traversiere zu spielen* (Berlin, 1752; 3rd edn, 1789/*R*1953); trans. E. R. Reilly as *On Playing the Flute* (London and New York, 1966), p. 120

3 R. Gandolfi, *Appunti intorno al clarinetto compilati ad uso delle scuole del R. Istituto musicale di Firenze* (Florence, 1887); W. Altenburg, *Die Klarinette* (Heilbronn, 1904)

4 O. W. Street, 'The clarinet and its music', *Proceedings of the Musical Association*, 42 (1915–16), pp. 89–115

5 A. Carse, *Musical Wind Instruments* (London, 1939/*R*1965), pp. 149–50

6 *Grove's Dictionary of Music and Musicians*, 5th edn (London, 1954), vol. II, p. 318, article 'clarinet'

7 O. Kroll, *Die Klarinette* (Kassel, 1965), Eng. trans. H. Morris, ed. A. Baines (London, 1968)

8 Orchestral clarinets were routinely changed by means of alternative joints (*corps de rechange*) from B♭ to A and from C to B (the latter specified in *Idomeneo* and *Così fan tutte*). Basset clarinets and basset horns associated with Mozart are discussed in Chapter 7.

9 In discussing a nineteenth-century reed, Shackleton notes its thinness at the heel, with the consequence that the active part of the reed included some of the harder, outer part of the cane.

10 C. Lawson and R. Stowell, *The Historical Performance of Music: An Introduction* (Cambridge, 1999)

11 N. Harnoncourt, *Baroque Music Today* (London, 1988), pp. 14–15

2 Historical considerations

1 This proposition has recently been proved by performers working within repertory where primary recorded evidence does exist, such as the orchestral style in Elgar's recordings from the 1920s and 1930s.

2 For example, see C. Lawson, *The Chalumeau in Eighteenth-Century Music* (Ann Arbor, 1981); A. R. Rice, *The Baroque Clarinet* (Oxford, 1992); C. Lawson, 'Single reeds before 1750', in Lawson (ed.), *The Cambridge Companion to the Clarinet* (Cambridge, 1995), pp. 1–15.

3 D. Schubart, *Ideen zu einer Ästhetik der Tonkunst* [1784–5] (Vienna, 1806), p. 326

4 J. G. Doppelmayr, *Historische Nachricht von den Nürnbergischen Mathematicis und Künstlern* (Nuremberg, 1730), p. 305

5 Ekkehard Nickel, *Die Holzblasinstrumentenbau in der freien Reichsstadt Nürnberg* (Munich, 1971), p. 214

6 In 1710 clarinets were among the instruments ordered from Jacob Denner by the Duke of Gronsfeld in Nuremberg. These are found in a document in the Nuremberg Staatsarchiv (Stadtrechnungsbeleg Repertorium 54a II, No. 1282)

7 C. Lawson, 'The chalumeau in the works of Fux', in H. White (ed.), *Johann Joseph Fux and the Music of the Austro-Italian Baroque* (Aldershot, 1992), pp. 78–94. Though much of this music remains inaccessible, two of Fux's operas (*Julo Ascanio* and *Pulcheria)* and two oratorios (*La fede sacrilega nella morte del Precursor S. Giovanni Battista* and *La donna forte nella madre de' sette Maccabei*) including chalumeaux have been published as part of a collected edition. In addition, J. H. Van der Meer, *Johann Joseph Fux als Opernkomponist* (Bilthoven, 1961) illustrates numbers with chalumeau from *Julo Ascanio* and *La decima fatica d'Ercole.*

8 E. F. Schmid, 'Gluck–Starzer–Mozart', *Zeitschrift für Musik*, 104 (1937), pp. 1198–1209

9 The title page of the Dittersdorf and extract from the chalumeau part are reproduced in Lawson (ed.), *The Cambridge Companion to the Clarinet*, p. 9.

10 Fasch Concerto FWV L: B1, Novello 120735 (1992). Three of Vivaldi's concertos, RV555, RV558 and RV579, have parts for tenor 'salmoè' and a sonata RV779 for violin, oboe and organ has an optional (tenor) chalumeau.

11 See C. Lawson, 'Telemann and the chalumeau', *Early Music*, 9 (1981), pp. 312–19; 'Graupner and the chalumeau', *Early Music*, 11 (1983), pp. 209–16.

12 The music of this exquisite aria may be found in an appendix to Chrysander's nineteeth-century Collected Edition. It has been recorded on Hyperion CDA66950.

13 J. Adlung, *Anleitung zu der musikalischen Gelahrtheit* (Erfurt, 1758/R1953), p. 588

14 See T. E. Hoeprich, 'Finding a clarinet for the three concertos by Vivaldi', *Early Music*, 11 (1983), pp. 60–4.

15 J. F. B. C. Majer, *Museum Musicum Theoretico Practicum* (Schwäbisch Hall,

1732/*R*1954); J. P. Eisel, *Musicus Autodidaktos* (Erfurt, 1738/*R*1976). The fingering charts are reproduced by Rice, *The Baroque Clarinet*, pp. 65, 69.

16 See the discussion in Chapter 4; also T. E. Warner, *An Annotated Bibliography of Woodwind Instruction Books, 1600–1830* (Detroit, 1967): J. X. Lefèvre, *Méthode de clarinette* (Paris, 1802/*R*1974): J. G. H. Backofen, *Anweisung zur Klarinette, nebst einer kurzen Abhandlung über das Bassett-Horn* (Leipzig, c. 1803/*R*1986).

17 See the discussion in Chapter 4 and also D. Charlton, 'Classical clarinet technique: documentary approaches', *Early Music*, 16 (1988), pp. 396–406.

18 For the principal issues see C. Lawson, *Mozart: Clarinet Concerto* (Cambridge, 1996); see also the Mozart Quintet case study in Chapter 6 and discussion of basset horn and basset clarinet in Chapter 7.

19 J. F. Schink, *Litterarische Fragmente* (Graz, 1785), p. 286

20 See E. Hess, 'Anton Stadler's "Musik Plan"', *Mozart-Jahrbuch* (1962), pp. 37–54, and P. Poulin, 'A view of eighteenth-century musical life and training: Anton Stadler's "Musick Plan"', *Music and Letters*, 71 (1990), pp. 215–24.

21 D. G. Türk, *Clavierschule* (Leipzig and Halle, 1789: Eng trans. Lincoln, NB and London, 1982)

22 K. Opperman, *Repertory of the Clarinet* (New York, 1960); E. Brixel, *Klarinetten-Bibliographie I* (Wilhelmshaven, 1978); G. Dobrée, 'A list of music for the clarinet', in F. Thurston, *Clarinet Technique* (Oxford, 1985, 4th rev. edn). See also J. Rees-Davies, 'The development of the clarinet repertoire', in Lawson (ed.), *The Cambridge Companion to the Clarinet*, pp. 75–91. We have already noted that in early Romantic repertory clarinets with ten or so keys by the great Dresden maker Heinrich Grenser have proved popular models for replicas; one of his clients was the celebrated Finnish clarinettist Bernhard Crusell.

23 H. Berlioz, *Grand traité d'instrumentation et d'orchestration modernes Op. 10* (Paris, 1843; Eng. trans., London, 1858)

24 C. Baermann, *Vollständige Clarinett-Schule*, 2 vols. (Offenbach, 1864–75)

25 A useful source for unusual repertory of this period is B. C. Tuthill, 'The clarinet in chamber music', in *Cobbett's Cyclopaedic Survey of Chamber Music* (Oxford, 1929/*R*1963), vol. I, pp. 279–82. A handful of sonatas pre-dates Brahms's Op. 120, including those by Prout, Swinnerton Heap and Draeseke. There are sets of character pieces by Gade, Reinecke, Stanford and Winding, *inter alia*.

26 There are English tutors from various parts of the nineteenth century, including Willman (1826) and Lazarus (1881).

27 H. Klosé, *Méthode pour servir à l'enseignement de la clarinette à anneaux mobiles, et de celle à 13 clés* (Paris, 1843)

28 For example, Wagner was in no doubt that in Beethoven's symphonies valved trumpets and horns should be used rather than their natural precursors; he re-

wrote their parts to remove any supposed limitations. On the other hand, Berlioz described the use of valves for stopped notes in Beethoven as a dangerous abuse; this is of special significance because he also enthuses about modern developments, such as Adolphe Sax's improvements to the clarinet and the newly devised Boehm flute. At a similar period Gleich claimed that the use of valves in Weber and Beethoven was a 'vandalismus'. *Grove's Dictionary of Music and Musicians*, [1st edn] (London, 1879) merely noted that both natural and valved instruments had their advantages.

29 Article 'oboe', *Grove 1*, vol. II, p. 487

30 R. Vollstedt, *Clarinettenschule zum Selbstunterricht* (Hamburg, n.d.), cited by K. Birsak, *Die Klarinette: Eine Kulturgeschichte* (Buchloe, 1992), p. 9

31 Baermann, *Vollständige Clarinett-Schule*, p. 33

32 F.-A. Gevaert, *Nouveau traité d'instrumentation et d'orchestration modernes* (Paris, 1885), p. 92

33 R. Strauss, *Instrumentationslehre* (Leipzig, 1905; Eng. trans. New York, 1948) [=Berlioz's *Grand traité*, rev. and exp.]; C. Forsyth, *Orchestration* (London, 1914)

34 J. Brymer, *Clarinet* (London, 1976), pp. 162–3

35 For example vols. I and II of *The Historical Recordings*, Clarinet Classics CC0005, CC0010

36 J. Levin in *Die Musik* (1926), quoted by Joseph Szigeti, *Szigeti on the Violin* (London, 1969), p. 176 and cited by R. Philip, *Early Recordings and Musical Style* (Cambridge, 1992), p. 218

37 F. G. Rendall, 'English and foreign wood-wind players and makers', *Music and Letters*, 12 (1931), p. 149

3 Equipment

1 See N. Shackleton, 'The development of the clarinet', in Lawson (ed.), *The Cambridge Companion to the Clarinet*, pp. 16–32.

2 The lack of standardisation is documented in detail in *The New Grove Dictionary of Music and Musicians* (London, 1980), article 'pitch'.

3 R. Maunder, 'Viennese wind-instrument makers, 1700-1800', *The Galpin Society Journal*, 51 (1998), p. 185. In making arrangements for Clara Schumann to hear his Clarinet Sonatas Op. 120, Brahms wrote to her in a celebrated letter: 'I have to tell you something which will cause us both a little annoyance. Mühlfeld will be sending you his tuning fork, so that the grand piano with which he is to play may be tuned to it. His clarinet only allows him to yield very little to other instruments.' See B. Litzmann (ed.), *Letters of Clara Schumann and Johannes Brahms 1853–1896*, 2 vols. (London, 1927), vol. II, p. 266.

4 The square flat leather pad gave way to the round stuffed variety in the first decade or so of the nineteenth century.

5 Shackleton, 'The development of the clarinet', p. 17

6 According to J. K. Rohn in *Nomenclator Artifex, et Mechanicus* (Prague, 1768). In the 1776 supplement to the *Encyclopédie*, F. D. Castilon observed, 'At the time of writing there is in Berlin a musician who plays a clarinet with six keys, in which he plays in all the tonalities. It has already been shown that four keys cause difficulties; how much worse it must be with six!' See E. Halfpenny, 'Castilon on the clarinet', *Music and Letters*, 35 (1954), pp. 332–8.

7 This illustration is reproduced in Lawson (ed.), *The Cambridge Companion to the Clarinet*, p. 138.

8 H. Grenser, 'Bemerkungen über eine neue Erfindung zur Vervollkommung der Flöte', *Allgemeine musikalische Zeitung*, 13 (1811), pp. 775–8

9 G. B. Shaw, *Music in London, 1890–4*, 3 vols. (London, 1931/R1973), vol. I, p. 96, as cited by Baines, *Woodwind Instruments*, p. 332

10 Writing under very different conditions from our own, Fröhlich recommended a used instrument for preference, on the grounds that it would speak more easily than a new one and would be already broken in. He adds that one is not in danger of finding the notes out of tune, as is the case with a new instrument. Also, new boxwood often cracks or moves. On the other hand, Backofen (p. 4) remarked that the bore of a used clarinet might have developed a fine mould blocking the pores of the wood and therefore new instruments were to be preferred.

11 C. Lawson, 'An investigation of clarinets and their makers', *Early Music Today*, 6 (December 1996 – January 1997), pp. 20–3

12 When notes accompanying a recording claim that it is played on period instruments, this can often mask a variety of practical expedients with respect to equipment, notwithstanding an underlying historical perspective.

13 Lawson (ed.), *The Cambridge Companion to the Clarinet*, p. 16

14 A.Vanderhagen, *Méthode nouvelle et raisonnée pour la clarinette* (Paris, *c.* 1785/R 1972), p. 3

15 *Metodo facilissimo per Imparare a ben suonare il clarinetto con quelle intelligenze necessarie, e perfette comunicative opportune ad'eseguire qualunque suonata con due dimostrazioni per il regolamento delle dita* (Florence, *c.* 1815)

16 Backofen, *Anweisung*, p. 3

17 *Ibid.*, p. 4

18 Fröhlich, *Vollständige theoretisch-praktische Musikschule*, pp. 9–11

19 His advice to soak a reed that has not been played for some time is perhaps more useful to today's players.

20 E. Planas, 'Oiling the wood', *Clarinet & Saxophone*, 8/1 (1983), pp. 9–11

21 Cited from the translation in Poulin, 'A view of eighteenth-century musical life', p. 219

22 *Metodo facilissimo,* p. 8

4 Playing historical clarinets

1 See Rice, *The Baroque Clarinet,* p. 139. Accompanying the engraving is a short text, an English translation of which reads: 'When the trumpet call is all too loud, the clarinet does serve to please, eschewing both the high and lowest sound, it varies gracefully and thus attains the prize. Wherefore the noble spirit enamoured of this reed, instruction craves and plays assiduously'; translation from Kroll, *The Clarinet,* p. 51. See also the front cover of the present book.

2 *The Clarinet Instructor, by which playing on that instrument is rendered easy . . .* (London, *c.* 1780), facing p. 2

3 For example 'Holyoke's Complete Scale for the Clarionett', in *The World of Music,* 1/11 (1840), p. 88

4 The latest Italian edition of Lefèvre's work is Alamiro Giampieri, *Metodo per clarinetto* (Milan, 1939)

5 Backofen, *Anweisung,* p. 4

6 Fröhlich, 'Vom Clarinett', *Vollständige theoretisch-praktische Musikschule,* pp. 7–35

7 *Ibid.,* p. 13

8 Klosé, *Méthode,* p. 1

9 Baermann, *Vollständige Clarinett-Schule,* trans. G. Langenus as *Complete Method for Clarinet Op. 63* (New York, 1918)

10 Baermann, *Vollständige Clarinett-Schule,* p. 5

11 Klosé, *Méthode,* p. 3. As can be deduced from his explanations of articulation, Klosé's 'lightness' of tongue refers to agility rather than the exclusive use of soft tongue strokes.

12 Reed position here refers to the placement of the reed under the top lip – reed-above – or on the bottom lip – reed-below. For a description of various terms adopted by previous writers to describe reed-position, see A. R. Rice, 'A history of the clarinet to 1820', Ph.D. thesis (Claremont Graduate School, Claremont, 1987), pp. 108–9

13 See Charlton, 'Classical clarinet technique', p. 396

14 I. Müller, *Méthode pour la nouvelle clarinette et clarinette-alto* (Paris, *c.* 1821), p. 23

15 Meissner held this post during the first twenty-two years of Fröhlich's life. See Ulrich Rau, 'Philipp Meißner, ein Klarinettenvirtuose des 18. Jahrhunderts', *Die Klarinette,* 1/4 (1987), pp. 26–7.

16 Ferdinando Sebastiani, *Metodo per clarinetto* (Naples, 1855), p. 7

17 See Ingrid Pearson, ' "Verfolgt vom Klang der Klarinette seines Vaters" – über Blatt-Position, Ferruccio Busoni und die Klarinette im Italien des 19. Jahrhunderts', *Tibia: Magazin für Holzbläser*, 24 (1999), pp. 605–11

18 Both Sebastiani and Labanchi mention tongued articulation exclusively.

19 Fröhlich, *Vollständige theoretisch-praktische Musikschule*, p. 13

20 F. Berr, *Traité complet de clarinette à quatorze clefs* (Paris, 1836), p. 2

21 Several mouthpieces for mid nineteenth-century German instruments survive overlaid with silver on the beak and rails.

22 Baermann, *Clarinett-Schule*, p. 6

23 Fröhlich, *Vollständige theoretisch-praktische Musikschule*, p. 14

24 *Ibid.*, p. 20

25 Müller, *Méthode*, p. 24. The combination of an unvoiced or voiced consonant and vowel has been used by most commentators to approximate the appropriate annunciation for various articulatory effects.

26 Schneider and Detouches, *Nouvelle méthode de clarinette* (Paris, c. 1840), p. 12

27 Compare the clarinet's wedged notes in the first movement of Brahms's Clarinet Quintet with those marked with dots in the final movement.

28 A. R. Rice, 'Clarinet fingering charts, 1732–1816', *The Galpin Society Journal*, 37 (1984), pp. 16–41

29 Lefèvre, *Méthode*, p. 6

30 Vanderhagen, *Méthode nouvelle*, p. 13. He also makes a useful suggestion regarding another trill between registers, that of c''' to d'''.

31 An article by Michaelis in the *Allgemeine musikalische Zeitung* of 1808 (vol. 25, dated 16 March, column 387) advocated that clarinets have at least nine keys.

32 Recent research suggests that others were also involved in the development of this instrument; see Nicholas Shackleton and Albert Rice, 'César Janssen and the transmission of Müller's 13-keyed clarinet in France', *The Galpin Society Journal*, 52 (1999), pp. 183–94.

33 Müller, *Méthode*, p. 2

34 Klosé, *Méthode*, p. 31

35 Vanderhagen, *Méthode nouvelle*, p. 11

36 Klosé, *Méthode*, p. 82

37 *Ibid.*, p. 84

38 *Ibid.*, p. 91

39 Baermann, *Clarinett-Schule*, p. 26

40 *Ibid.*

41 These sonatas have appeared in modern publications by Schott, Oxford University Press, Richli, Galaxy and others.

42 Klosé, *Méthode*, pp. 28–30
43 *Ibid.*, p. 18
44 *Ibid.*, p. 24
45 Lefèvre, *Méthode*, p. 16, and Baermann, *Clarinett-Schule.*, p. 29
46 Letter to Georg Henschel quoted by Philip, *Early Recordings and Musical Style*, p. 218. See also page 96 of the present book.
47 Baermann, *Clarinett-Schule*, p. 29
48 Klosé, *Méthode*, p. 57

5 The language of musical style

1 Fröhlich, *Vollständige theoretisch-praktische Musikschule*, pp. 7–8
2 Lefèvre, *Mèthode*, pp. 13–14
3 L. Mozart, *Versuch einer gründlichen Violinschule* (Augsburg, 1756/R 1976); trans. E. Knocker (Oxford, 1948), pp. 123–4
4 *Ibid.*, Eng. trans., p. 46
5 Quantz, *Versuch*, p. 185
6 Lefèvre, *Méthode*, p. 20. On temperament see Lawson and Stowell (eds.), The *Historical Performance of Music;* Brown and Sadie (eds.), *Performance Practice: Music after 1600* (London, 1989); C. Folkers, 'Playing in tune on a baroque flute', *Traverso*, 10 (1998), pp. 1–3.
7 Baermann, *Clarinett-Schule*, p. 1
8 Türk, *Clavierschule*, pp. 332–3
9 *Ibid.*, pp. 310–11
10 *Ibid.*, p. 313
11 C. Czerny, *Über den richtigen Vortrag der sämtlichen Beethoven'schen Klavierwerke* (Vienna, 1846), p. 11
12 See H. C. Robbins Landon and D. Mitchell, *The Mozart Companion* (London, 1965), p. 33, n. 3.
13 P. Baillot, *L'Art du violon: nouvelle méthode* (Paris, 1834), p. 268
14 G. Kaiser (ed.), *Carl Maria von Weber, Sämmtliche Schriften* (Berlin, 1908), quoted in S. Morgenstern (ed.), *Composers on Music* (London, 1958), pp. 100–1
15 J. A. Fuller Maitland, *Joseph Joachim* (London and New York, 1905), pp. 29–30

6 Case studies in ensemble music

1 The aria 'Par che mi nasca' in the autograph of Handel's opera *Tamerlano* (1724) appears in two versions, in G major with flutes and violins and in C major with cornetti and violins. A copyist's score in the Granville Collection (British Library

Eg. 2920) has the C major version with clarinets replacing the cornetti. The rubric *Clar. 1/Clar. 2* has been taken to indicate clarinets rather than trumpets both from the style of the music and the presence of flutes in the G major version. Scholars have disagreed as to whether this alternative scoring was sanctioned by Handel. The manuscript was copied for Bernard Granville (1709–75), a friend and admirer of the composer, and it does seem quite likely that the copy dates from after Handel's death, when the clarinet had a regular place in the London opera orchestra. On the other hand, J. P. Larsen, *Handel's Messiah: Origins, Compositions, Sources* (New York, 1972), pp. 211–12, states that the Granville copies were completed around 1744–5.

2 The first thirty-two bars of the autograph are reproduced in the Hallische Händel-Ausgabe, vol. IV/15 (Kassel, 1979), p. xvii.

3 For example, J. A. Fuller Maitland and A. H. Mann, *Catalogue of the Music in the Fitzwilliam Museum, Cambridge* (Cambridge, 1893), p. 221: 'The Concertino parts complete . . . of an "overture" in five movements . . . The string parts of this work are not at present forthcoming: it is to be hoped that they will be found in some of the Libraries containing Handel's MSS., so as to enable the performance and publication of this important composition to be undertaken. It was probably written about 1740.'

4 See P. Weston, *Clarinet Virtuosi of the Past* (London, 1971), pp. 17–28 and Rice, *The Baroque Clarinet*, pp. 144–8. Both authors reproduce an announcement in the *Dublin Mercury* for Mr Charles's first concert in Dublin on 12 May 1742.

5 R. B. Chatwin, 'Handel and the clarinet', *The Galpin Society Journal*, 3 (1950), pp. 3–8

6 B. Baselt in W. and M. Eisen (eds.), *Händel-Handbuch* , 5 vols. to date (Kassel, 1978–), vol. II, p. 208. Bound in the same volume are six pages of the well-known concerto in D, No. 5 of the Twelve Grand Concertos, also used as the *Overture to St. Cecilia's Day*; page 12 of the manuscript bears the signature 'G. F. Handel, Oct. 10, 1739'.

7 In the Haas score these are respectively bars 38, 50 and 60–4.

8 Equivalent to bar 60 in the Haas edition

9 This clarinet is illustrated in Lawson (ed.), *The Cambridge Companion to the Clarinet*, p. 7. See also the copy in Fig. 3.2 on p. 33 of the present volume.

10 Chatwin, 'Handel and the clarinet', p. 7

11 Rice, *The Baroque Clarinet*, p. 109

12 J. F. Agricola, *Anleitung zur Singkunst* (Berlin, 1757); trans. J. C. Baird as *Introduction to the Art of Singing* (Cambridge, 1995), p. 158; C. P. E. Bach, *Versuch über die wahre Art das Clavier zu spielen*, 2 vols. (Berlin, 1753–62); trans. W. J. Mitchell as *Essay on the True Art of Playing Keyboard Instruments* (New York,

1949), pp. 157–8; L. Mozart, *Versuch*, Eng. trans., pp. 41–2. See also Quantz, *Versuch*, Eng. trans., p. 67.

13 The *Ouverture* for two clarinets and horn, however, offers something of an ambiguous case, the Hallische Händel-Ausgabe, p. x, arguing (unconvincingly, in the present writer's opinion) that because of the nature of the rhythmic detail, no over-dotting is required.

14 R. T. Dart, *The Interpretation of Music* (London, 1954), pp. 80–1

15 See M. Collins, 'The performance of triplets in the seventeenth and eighteenth centuries', *Journal of the American Musicological Society*, 19 (1966), pp. 281–328.

16 The quartet is reproduced in Rice, *The Baroque Clarinet*, pp. 129–32.

17 'Faute de clarinettes, on pourra les Exécuter avec deux Hautbois, Flûtes ou Violons.' See *ibid.*, p. 133.

18 See P. Weston, *More Clarinet Virtuosi of the Past* (London, 1977), pp. 199, 102, 204 and 224.

19 Gradenwitz, 'The beginnings of clarinet literature: notes on a clarinet concerto by Joh. Stamitz', *Music and Letters*, 17 (1936), pp. 145–50. He notes (p. 146) that the virtuoso Joseph Beer played a 'Concerto pour clarinette de Stamitz' at the Concerts Spirituels on 2 February 1772. This (however) was probably a concerto by Karl Stamitz; according to Weston (*More Clarinet Virtuosi*, p. 44), his First Concerto was definitely played on that occasion.

20 Lawson, *Mozart: Clarinet Concerto*, p. 78

21 The middle joints of a four-keyed clarinet *c.* 1760 by the Brussels maker G. A. Rottenburgh are illustrated in Lawson (ed.), *The Cambridge Companion to the Clarinet*, p. 23.

22 Clarinet in B♭ by Thomas Collier, London, 1770: Keighley, Cliffe Castle Museum, No. 9110

23 In contrast, the movement also contains short, unaccented appoggiaturas, as at bars 57, 62–3.

24 Quantz, *Versuch*, Eng. trans., p. 185

25 P. L. Poulin, 'Anton Stadler's basset clarinet: recent discoveries in Riga', *Journal of the American Musical Instrument Society*, 22 (1996), p. 126

26 *The Letters of Mozart and his Family*, trans. E. Anderson (London, 1938; rev. 2 vols. 1966), vol. II, p. 937

27 J. Kratochvíl, 'Betrachtungen über die Urfassung des Konzerts für Klarinette und des Quintetts für Klarinette und Streicher von W. A. Mozart', *Internationale Konferenz über das Leben und Werk W. A. Mozarts 1956* (Prague, 1958), pp. 262–71; 'Ist die heute gebräuchliche Fassung des Klarinettenkonzerts und des Klarinettenquintetts von Mozart authentisch?' *Beiträge zur Musikwissen-*

schaft, 2 (1960), pp. 27–34. Kratochvíl was responsible for the reconstructed text of Mozart's Clarinet Concerto when in 1951 a basset clarinet version was revived by Milan Kostohryz's pupil Josef Janous.

28 On the twentieth-century revival of the basset clarinet see Lawson, *Mozart: Clarinet Concerto*, pp. 50–1. Both these designs sometimes incorporate a curved barrel. The author's basset clarinet, made by Daniel Bangham in 1988 and used for the Mozart Concerto recording, Nimbus NI5228, has in addition a slight angle between joints, resembling the anonymous clarinet in Paris, Muséee de la Musique 2646 980, 2. 566.

29 F. Bertuch, 'Wiener Kunstnachrichten', *Journal des Luxus und Moden*, 16 (October 1801), pp. 543–4

30 A description of the letter appears in the antiquarian Hans Schneider's Katalog Nr. 308 (Tutzing) of autographs of musicians, p. 76.

31 G. Dazeley, 'The original text of Mozart's Clarinet Concerto', *Music Review*, 9 (1948), pp. 166–72

32 Türk, *Clavierschule*, Eng. trans., pp. 360–1

33 Quantz, *Versuch*, Eng. trans., p. 284

34 See Poulin, 'A view of eighteenth-century musical life', p. 220.

35 Weston, *Clarinet Virtuosi of the Past*, pp. 127–8

36 Weston, *More Clarinet Virtuosi of the Past*, p. 129

37 Cited in Weston, *Clarinet Virtuosi of the Past*, p. 78

38 For example, the author's recording on Classic FM 75605 57019 2 (1998) has the timings 8'41", 7'10" and 6'28".

39 D. Cairns, trans and ed., *The Memoirs of Hector Berlioz, Member of the French Institute, including his travels in Italy, Germany, Russia and England, 1803–65* (New York, 1975), p. 264. When Sir George Smart heard Weber conduct *Der Freischütz* in Dresden, the string section was 5–5–2–2–2. See H. B. Cox and C. L. E. Cox, *Leaves from the Journals of Sir George Smart* (London, 1907), pp. 139–40.

40 Ignaz Moscheles, *Recent Music and Musicians as Described in the Diaries and Correspondence*, ed. his wife, trans. A. D. Coleridge (New York, 1970 from first edn, 1873), pp. 82–3

41 Here Weber's phrase marking extends across two quaver rests in the clarinet part in bar 81.

42 The Viennese premières of both the Trio and the Quintet were given by clarinet-tists other than Mühlfeld. On 17 December 1891 the Trio was played by Adalbert Syrinek, principal clarinet of the Vienna Philharmonic, with Brahms and cellist Ferdinand Hellmesberger. Later in his career, Mühlfeld formed a trio with two

Meiningen colleagues, the conductor and pianist Wilhelm Berger and cellist Karl Piening.

43 M. MacDonald, *Brahms* (London, 1990), pp. 366–7

44 For example, the four crotchet beats from bar 222³ to 223² in the first movement are absent in the autograph, making the coda a bar shorter.

45 N. Shackleton and K. Puddy, 'Mühlfeld's clarinets', *Clarinet & Saxophone,* 14/1 (1989), pp. 26–7. See also J. Seggelke, 'Die Baermann-Ottensteiner-Klarinette im musikgeschichtlichen Kontext', *Rohrblatt,* 11/1 (1996), pp. 2–5.

46 See M. Hauptmann in *Jahrbuch für musikalische Wissenschaft,* 1 (1863), p. 22 and A. von Dommer, *H. C. Koch's Musikalisches Lexicon* (Heidelberg, 1865), p. 100.

47 On Mühlfeld's playing, see C. Lawson, *Brahms: Clarinet Quintet* (Cambridge, 1998), especially pp. 68–71: Street, 'The clarinet and its music', 42 (1916), pp. 89–115; F. G. Rendall, 'The clarinet in England', *Proceedings of the Musical Association,* 68 (1942), pp. 55–86 and *The Clarinet* (London, 1954; rev. 3rd edn by P. Bate, 1971); A. Baines, *Woodwind Instruments and their History* (London, 1957, 3rd edn, 1967); Weston, *Clarinet Virtuosi of the Past*; discussions and correspondence in *Clarinet & Saxophone,* 13/4 (1988) and 14/1 (1989).

48 Joachim (Joseph Joachim and Andreas Moser, *Violinschule,* 3 vols. (Berlin, 1902–5), vol. II, p. 96a) remarked, 'As a means borrowed from the human voice . . . the use and manner of executing the portamento must come naturally under the same rules which hold good in vocal art.'

49 J. W. Finson, 'Performing practice in the late nineteenth century, with special reference to the music of Brahms', *The Musical Quarterly,* 70/4 (1984), p. 463

50 A photograph of the Wendling Quartet with Mühlfeld *c.* 1899 is reproduced on p. 43 of Lawson, *Brahms: Clarinet Quintet.*

51 See R. Winter, 'The 19th Century: Keyboards', in Brown and Sadie (eds.), *Performance Practice: Music after 1600,* pp. 367–8.

52 On the Baermann system the L2 and L4 touch-pieces for f′ present a challenge to technical fluency, as does the Rth alternative lever for f♯/c♯″. Both were abandoned in the subsequent refinement of the German system by Oehler. Baermann's provision of a R1 side-key for e♭′/b♭″ offers a useful advantage over the plain Albert system, but the latter's 'patent c♯″' (whereby the L4 lever depressed without R4 produces c♯″ instead of b′) redresses the balance in no small measure. For more details of the Baermann system and of its mechanism, see Lawson, *Brahms: Clarinet Quintet,* pp. 10–11, and 91–2. For illustrations, see Weston, *Clarinet Virtuosi of the Past,* plates 24 and 25; also *Clarinet & Saxophone,* 14/1 (1989), front cover and pp. 26–7.

53 R. H. Schauffler, *The Unknown Brahms* (New York, 1933), p. 180

54 J. Bloch, *Methodik des Violinspiels und Violinunterrichts* (Strasbourg, [1903]), p. 347

7 Related family members

1 See, for example, A. R. Rice, 'The clarinette d'amour and basset horn', *The Galpin Society Journal*, 39 (1986), pp. 97–124.

2 See N. Shackleton in Lawson (ed.), *The Cambridge Companion to the Clarinet*, p. 32.

3 See especially Michael Harris's remarks in Lawson (ed.), *The Cambridge Companion to the Clarinet*, pp. 67–8.

4 The years 1783–5 alone account for some thirteen works: KK436, 437, 438, 439, 346/439a, 439b, 452a, 477/479a, 411/484a, 484b, 484c, 410/484d and 484e.

5 A six-keyed basset horn of this design is described by J. G. L. von Wilke in his *Musikalisches Handwörterbuch* (Weimar, 1786) and a seven-keyed version by E. L. Gerber in his *Historisch-biographisches Lexicon der Tonkünstler* (Leipzig, 1790–2).

6 C. F. Cramer, *Magazin der Musik* (Hamburg, 1783), p. 654

7 In addition to the basset horns in G and F used by Mozart, they were also constructed in E, E♭ and D, according to J. G. Albrechtsberger's *Gründliche Anweisung zur Composition* (Leipzig, 1790).

8 J. F. von Schönfeld, *Jahrbuch der Tonkunst von Wien und Prag* (1796), p. 58

9 Significantly, however, Stadler's own *Terzetti* provide an *ossia* an octave higher whenever the note occurs in his lowest basset horn part.

10 For example, if a and b♭ in the chalumeau register are too high they can be lowered and at the same time vented by adding the right-hand little finger depressing both the f/c″ and a♭/e♭″ keys simultaneously. This can be useful advice for the opening basset horn 1 solo in the Adagio of Mozart's Serenade K361.

11 Reproduced in C. Lawson, 'The basset clarinet revived', *Early Music*, 15 (1987), pp. 487–501 and in Lawson (ed.), *The Cambridge Companion to the Clarinet*, p. 148

12 Backofen, *Anweisung*, p. 35

13 G. von Nissen, *Biographie W. A. Mozarts* (Leipzig, 1828), Anh. p. 17 No. 4

14 R. D. Levin, 'Das Klarinettenquintett B-Dur, KV Anh. 91/516c; ein Ergänzungsversuch', *Mozart-Jahrbuch* (1968–70), p. 320 and the preface to his completion, published by Nagels Verlag (Kassel, 1970).

15 See Lawson, *Mozart: Clarinet Concerto*, pp. 84–90.
16 *Ibid*, pp. 52–9. Pamela Weston's new edition is based on a contemporary arrange-
    ment by C. F. G. Schwencke for piano quintet, which may offer some clues as to
    original melodic contours and appropriate ornamentation. This version devel-
    ops some of the ideas first advanced by Arthur Ness, 'Some remarks concerning
    the basset clarinet and Mozart's Concerto in A major (KV 622)', M.A. thesis
    (Harvard University, 1961).
17 See Lawson, *Mozart : Clarinet Concerto*, pp. 77–8.

Select bibliography

Bach, C. P. E., *Versuch über die wahre Art das Clavier zu spielen*, 2 vols. (Berlin, 1753–62), trans. W. J. Mitchell as *Essay on the True Art of Playing Keyboard Instruments* (New York, 1949)

Backofen, J. G. H., *Anweisung zur Klarinette, nebst einer kurzen Abhandlung über das Bassett-Horn* (Leipzig, c. 1803/R1986)

Baermann, C., *Vollständige Clarinett-Schule* (Offenbach, 1864–75)

Baines, A., *Woodwind Instruments and their History* (London, 1957; 3rd edn, 1967/R1991)

Berr, F., *Traité complet de la clarinette à quatorze clefs* (Paris, 1836)

Birsak, K., *Die Klarinette: Eine Kulturgeschichte* (Buchloe, 1992, trans. G. Schamberger, 1994)

Blasius, F., *Nouvelle méthode de clarinette* (Paris, 1796/R1972)

Brymer, J., *Clarinet* (London, 1976)

Charlton, D., 'Classical clarinet technique: documentary approaches', *Early Music*, 16 (1988), pp. 396–406

Chatwin, R. B., 'Handel and the clarinet', *The Galpin Society Journal*, 3 (1950), pp. 3–8

Dazeley, G., 'The original text of Mozart's Clarinet Concerto', *Music Review*, 9 (1948), pp. 166–72

Finson, J. W., 'Performing practice in the late nineteenth century, with special reference to the music of Brahms', *The Musical Quarterly*, 70/4 (1984), pp. 457–75

Fröhlich, J., *Vollständige theoretisch-praktische Musikschule* (Bonn, 1810–11)

Gradenwitz, P., 'The beginnings of clarinet literature: notes on a clarinet concerto by Joh. Stamitz', *Music and Letters*, 17 (1936), pp. 145–50

Hacker, A., 'Mozart and the basset clarinet', *Musical Times*, 110 (1969), pp. 359–62

Haskell, H., *The Early Music Revival* (London, 1988)

Hoeprich, T. E., 'Finding a clarinet for the three concertos by Vivaldi', *Early Music*, 11 (1983), pp. 60–4

'Clarinet reed position in the 18th century', *Early Music*, 12 (1984), pp. 49–55

Klosé, H., *Méthode pour servir à l'enseignement de la clarinette à anneaux mobiles* (Paris, 1843)

Kroll, O., *Die Klarinette* (Kassel, 1965), trans. H. Morris, ed. A. Baines (London, 1968)

Langwill, L. G., *An Index of Wind-Instrument Makers* (Edinburgh, 1960; rev. enlarged 6th edn, 1980), rev. W. Waterhouse as *The New Langwill Index* (London, 1993)

Lawson, C., 'The chalumeau: independent voice or poor relation?' *Early Music*, 7 (1979), pp. 351–4

  The Chalumeau in Eighteenth-Century Music (Ann Arbor, 1981)

  'The authentic clarinet: tone and tonality', *Musical Times*, 124 (1983), pp. 357–8

  'The basset clarinet revived', *Early Music*, 15 (1987), pp. 487–501

  Mozart: Clarinet Concerto (Cambridge, 1996)

  Brahms: Clarinet Quintet (Cambridge, 1998)

Lawson, C. (ed.), *The Cambridge Companion to the Clarinet* (Cambridge, 1995)

Lawson, C., and Stowell, R., *The Historical Performance of Music: An Introduction* (Cambridge, 1999)

Lazarus, H., *New and Modern Method for the Clarinet* (London, 1881)

Leeson, D. N., and Whitwell, D., 'Concerning Mozart's Serenade for thirteen instruments, KV 361 (370a)', *Mozart-Jahrbuch* (1976–7), pp. 97–130

Lefèvre, J. X., *Méthode de clarinette* (Paris, 1802/R1974)

Longyear, R. M., 'Clarinet sonorities in early Romantic music', *Musical Times*, 124 (1983), pp. 224–6

Lyle, A., 'John Mahon's clarinet tutor', *The Galpin Society Journal*, 30 (1977), pp. 52–5

Maunder, R., 'Viennese wind-instrument makers, 1700–1800', *The Galpin Society Journal*, 51 (1998), p. 185

Mozart, L., *Versuch einer gründlichen Violinschule* (Augsburg, 1756/R1976), trans. E. Knocker (Oxford, 1948)

Müller, I., *Méthode pour la nouvelle clarinette et clarinette-alto* (Paris, c. 1821)

Philip, R., *Early Recordings and Musical Style* (Cambridge, 1992)

Poulin, P. L., 'The basset clarinet of Anton Stadler', *College Music Symposium*, 22 (1982), pp. 67–82

  'A view of eighteenth-century musical life and training: Anton Stadler's "Musik Plan"', *Music and Letters*, 71 (1990), pp. 215–24

  'Anton Stadler's basset clarinet: recent discoveries in Riga', *Journal of the American Musical Instrument Society*, 22 (1996), pp. 110–27

Quantz, J. J., *Versuch einer Anweisung die Flöte traversiere zu spielen* (Berlin, 1752; 3rd edn, 1789/R1953), trans. E. R. Reilly as *On Playing the Flute* (London and New York, 1966)

Rees-Davies, J., *Bibliography of the Early Clarinet* (Brighton, 1986)

Rendall, F. G., *The Clarinet* (London, 1954; rev. 3rd edn by P. Bate, 1971)

Rice, A. R., 'Clarinet fingering charts, 1732–1816', *The Galpin Society Journal*, 37 (1984), pp. 16–41

The Baroque Clarinet (Oxford, 1992)

Roeser, V., *Essai d'instruction à l'usage de ceux qui composent pour la clarinette et le cor* (Paris, 1764/R1972)

Shackleton, N., 'The earliest basset horns', *The Galpin Society Journal*, 40 (1987), pp. 2–23

Sherman, B. (ed), *Inside Early Music: Conversations with Performers* (Oxford, 1997)

Türk, D. G., *Clavierschule* (Leipzig and Halle, 1789), trans. Raymond Haggh as *School of Clavier Playing* (Lincoln, NB and London, 1982)

Vanderhagen, A., *Méthode nouvelle et raisonnée pour la clarinette* (Paris, c. 1785/R1972)

Warner, T. E., *An Annotated Bibliography of Woodwind Instruction Books, 1600–1830* (Detroit, 1967)

Weston, P., *Clarinet Virtuosi of the Past* (London, 1971)

More Clarinet Virtuosi of the Past (London, 1977)

Whistling, C. F., and Hofmeister, F., *Handbuch der musicalischen Literatur* (Leipzig, 1817, with ten supplements, 1818–27/R1975)

Willman, T. L. A., *A Complete Instruction Book for the Clarinet* (London, 1826)

Young, P. T., *4900 Historical Woodwind Instruments: An Inventory of 200 Makers in International Collections* (London, 1993)

Index